sovereign traces | volume 1

Not (Just) (An)Other

Edited by Gordon Henry Jr. and Elizabeth LaPensée

Makwa Enewed | East Lansing

♾ The paper used in this publication meets the minimum requirements of ANSI/NISO
Z39.48-1992 (R 1997) (Permanence of Paper).

SOVEREIGN
TRACES

Gordon Henry Jr. and Elizabeth LaPensée, *Series Editors*

Sovereign Traces, Volume 1: Not (Just) (An)Other | ISBN 978-1-938065-06-4
Edited by Gordon Henry Jr. and Elizabeth LaPensée

Michigan State University Press
East Lansing, Michigan 48823-5245

Makwa Enewed is an imprint of Michigan State University Press
East Lansing, Michigan 48823-5245

Printed and bound in the United States of America.

27 26 25 24 23 22 21 20 19 18   1 2 3 4 5 6 7 8 9 10

Library of Congress Control Number: 2017963073 | ISBN: 978-1-938065-06-4 (pbk.)

Book and cover design by Charlie Sharp, Sharp Des!gns, East Lansing, Michigan.
Cover artwork (excluding shell panels) by Elizabeth LaPensée.

g green
press
INITIATIVE

Michigan State University Press is a member of the Green Press Initiative
and is committed to developing and encouraging ecologically responsible
publishing practices. For more information about the Green Press Initiative and the use of
recycled paper in book publishing, please visit *www.greenpressinitiative.org.*

Visit Michigan State University Press at *www.msupress.org*

contents

beginnings and future imaginings

Initial discussions for the publication of this work began at the Native American Literature Symposium in 2013. At that time, Niigaanwewidam James Sinclair met with Julie Loehr, the assistant director of MSU Press, and me, to discuss the possibility of creating a graphic literature series for the MSU Press. MSU Press and the Sovereign Traces Series are indebted to Niigaan for his vision and effort in bringing forth the ideas and resources crucial to getting this collection off the ground. In the fall of the same year I applied for and received a HARP institutional research grant from the College of Arts and Letters and Michigan State University. That grant provided some financial support to move the project forward. With funds from the grant, MSU Press, Niigaan, and I commissioned graphic artists to produce work for adapted versions of extant, previously published works in Indigenous literature— both American and Canadian. At the same time, other grant funds went to writers who wanted to work with an artist of their choosing on new, unpublished work. After years of back-and-forth correspondence with writers and graphic artists, the collection floundered a bit, hung up in the details publishers, writers, editors, and editorial staff often navigate through to bring a multiple-sourced collection to print. For a while, we had the literature, the written content, complete and ready to go, but we lacked illustrations and the visual adaptations for a handful of stories and poems. Then we re-formed the editorial team for the collection and added Beth LaPensée as coeditor. The energy and connections Beth brought to the collection got us over the edge. She put us in touch with artists and illustrators who completed the work for the unadapted stories and poems, and she provided illustrations for one of the works included here as well as produced the cover art for collection. She continues the series on with *Sovereign Traces, Volume 2: Relational Constellation*, a comic collection about Indigenous love, forthcoming from MSU Press in partnership with Native Realities Press.

Future Sovereign Traces collections include comic adaptations of foundational American Indian law cases and a volume dedicated to dual-language versions of "traditional" Anishinaabe adisokan tribal stories. As with this volume, we see those future collections of illustrated literature as but part of an invested and marked commitment by MSU Press to the cultural continuance and to adaptive remembrance of the wealth of stories and the profound intellectual and imaginative cultural legacies of Indigenous people and communities.

not (just) (an)other

In the introduction to *The Remembered Earth*, an anthology of Native literature, published more than forty years ago, Geary Hobson, the editor of that collection, wrote:

> Native American literature certainly
> . . . is indeed much more than a
> "boom," or a "fad,"—to echo what
> certain literary scholars have said. It
> is renewal, it is continuance—and it
> is remembering. (2)

While the terms for discussing and critiquing Indigenous literature may have moved on from core themes Hobson associated with Native Lit to more contemporary critical memes of "decolonization," "sovereignty," "survivance," "resistance," "indigeneity," and "intersectionality"—those themes and memes, past and present, underscore the deep cultural connections and concerns of most of us who have roots and relatives in tribal communities and who have lived American Indian and First Nations studies over the years, before and since the publication of *The Remembered Earth*. That is, we recognize in the changing language and critical formations of contemporary academic discussions of Indigenous literature, Native writers' commitment to cultural continuance, as testament to the strength and resilience of tribal cultures and communities and as indicating the imaginative possibilities for the intergenerational transmission and renewal of timeless stories and cultural lifeways.

To be sure, since *The Remembered Earth* came out, the literary works of Native writers have made even more significant inroads into the nontribal readership spheres of American and Canadian popular culture, the hegemonic literary canon of North American letters, and the smaller, but significant, world of the concerns and curricula of academia. Most notably, the work of writers Louise Erdrich and Sherman Alexie stand out as generally well-known to a breadth of audiences throughout the world, making them among the most eminent writers in the Americas. Other widely known writers, such as Joy Harjo, Linda Hogan, N. Scott Momaday, James Welch, and Simon Ortiz, have forged a lasting influence in the larger body of American and international letters as well. Still others, like Gerald Vizenor have maintained, for decades, a strong academic readership and a lasting engagement with academic audiences in Europe.

But, of course, that is just part of the story. Hundreds of other, lesser-known North American Indigenous writers have contributed significant works of literature, in a multiplicity of genres and genre-hopping texts, to a diverse, continually growing body of literature by tribal people of North America. Further, that growing body of literature has produced extensions of the written work of many Native writers. Writing by North American Indigenous authors has been adapted to film, performed live with music and as spoken word, dramatized in theatre performance, recorded as audio and video for various electronic platforms and websites, and integrated into art installations, among other possibilities, comics included.

The foundational work of comic creators like Arigon Starr, Lee Francis IV, Jay Odjick, and Jon Proudstar have provided Indigenous writers, illustrators, colorists, and editors the opportunity to make what they love into what they do through the growing area of self-determined comics and graphic novels. The Indigenous Comic Con continues to bring communities together as the body of work from Native Realities Press and other publishers across North America reach more and more people. This inaugural collection uniquely contributes to this momentum through the Sovereign Traces series, which uniquely adapts short stories, poems, and excerpts by North American Indigenous writers into graphic representation.

By merging works of contemporary North American Indian literature with imaginative illustrations by U.S. and Canadian artists, this collection embodies yet another, unique, extended means for audiences to engage with works of Native Literature—the primary consideration as we moved toward developing and shaping this volume. We also hoped to bring new audiences to important, existing, Native writing, along with possibilities for reimagined readings of that writing. Thus, in the work that follows readers will find works of graphic literature, newly adapted from writing by American Indians and First Peoples. This collection also is singular in its inclusion of works of both poetry and fiction, as it marks further uniqueness by bringing together work of authors and artists from both Canada and the United States.

The series opens with *Not (Just) (An)Other*, a title echoing the closing comic "Just Another Naming Ceremony," which uses laughter as medicine. During the journey of experiencing these comics, through the grit of tribulations and darkness and to the brilliant splashes of realizations and color, this collection asserts itself as not just another. It shares the kind of stories that parallel our communities, the stories Auntie tells when no one else is around, the ones that keep it real.

sovereign traces

volume 1

Stephen Graham Jones, Ivena Baldwin Chair
of English at the University of Colorado–Boulder,
is the author of twenty-five books so far. Most
recent is the novella *Mapping the Interior* and the
comic book *My Hero*. Jones has been an NEA
Fellow and a Texas Writers League Fellow, and
he has won the Texas Institute of Letters Award
for Fiction, as well as the Independent Publishers
Multicultural Award. His areas of interest,
aside from fiction writing, are horror, science
fiction, fantasy, film, comic books, pop culture,
technology, and American Indian Studies. Jones
received his BA in English and Philosophy from
Texas Tech University (1994), his MA in English
from the University of North Texas (1996), and his
PhD from Florida State University (1998).

BUS LANE
BUS LANE
AND WE'RE NOT WEREWOLVES, OKAY?
CLEAR ON THAT?
WEREWOLF
SCHOOL PARKING ONLY
SON of A WEREWOLF

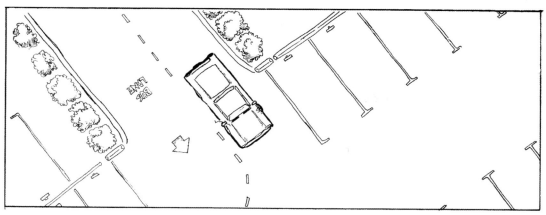

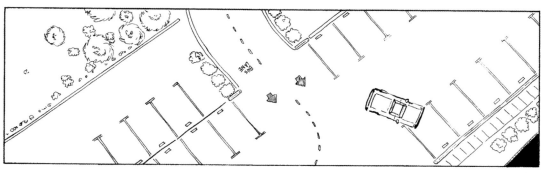

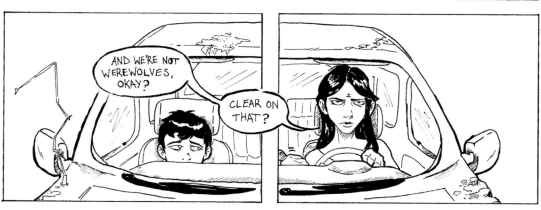

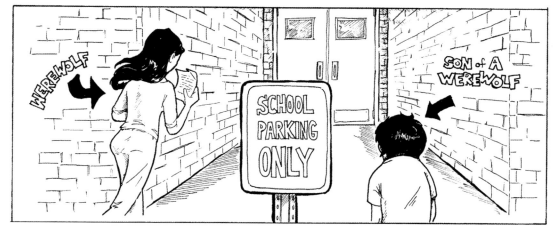

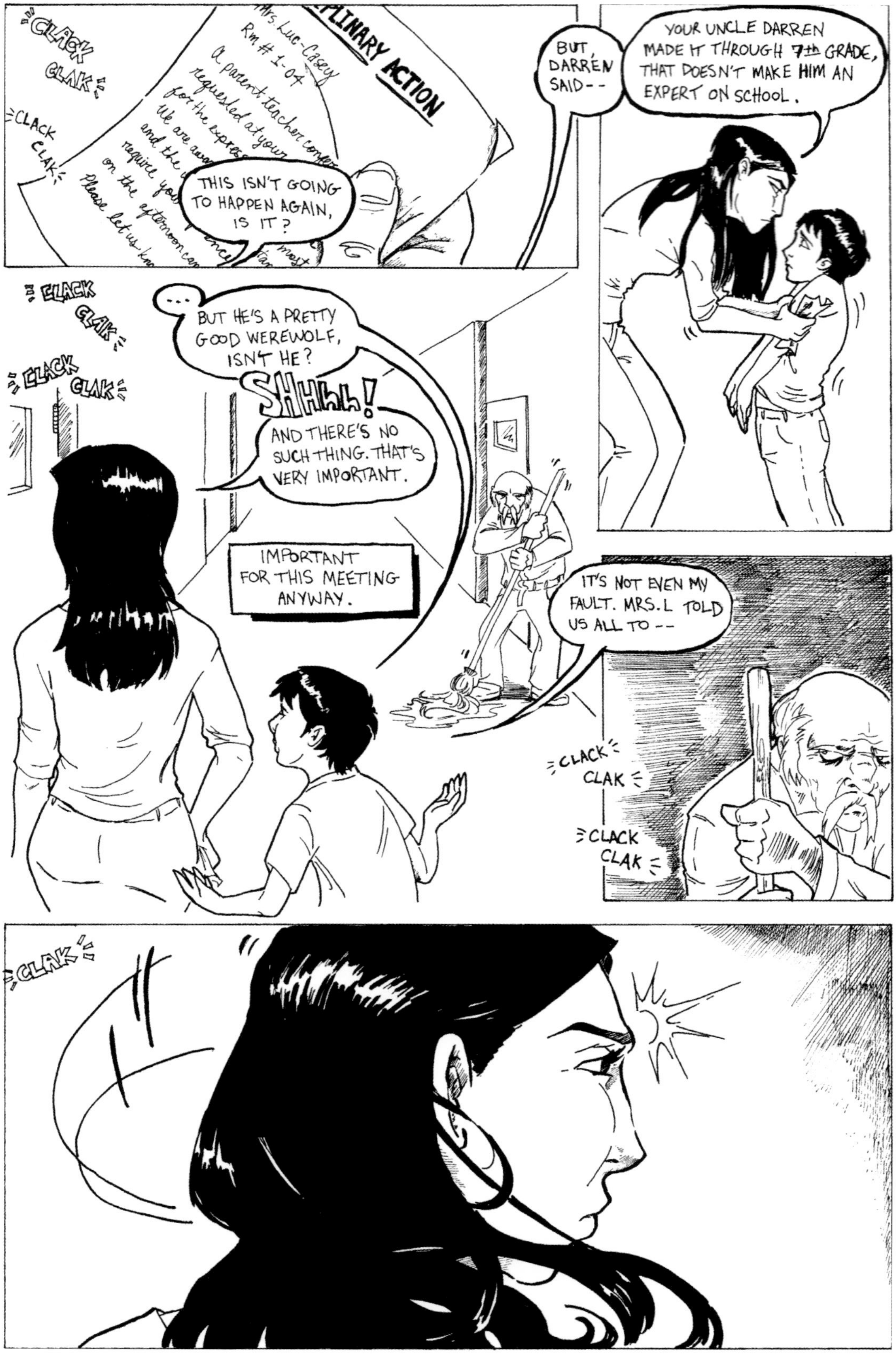
CLACK
CLAK
CLACK
CLAK
THIS ISN'T GOING TO HAPPEN AGAIN, IS IT?
BUT, DARREN SAID--
YOUR UNCLE DARREN MADE IT THROUGH 7th GRADE, THAT DOESN'T MAKE HIM AN EXPERT ON SCHOOL.
CLACK
CLAK
CLACK
CLAK
... BUT HE'S A PRETTY GOOD WEREWOLF, ISN'T HE?
SHHhh!
AND THERE'S NO SUCH THING. THAT'S VERY IMPORTANT.
IMPORTANT FOR THIS MEETING ANYWAY.
IT'S NOT EVEN MY FAULT. MRS. L TOLD US ALL TO --
CLACK
CLAK
CLACK
CLAK
CLAK

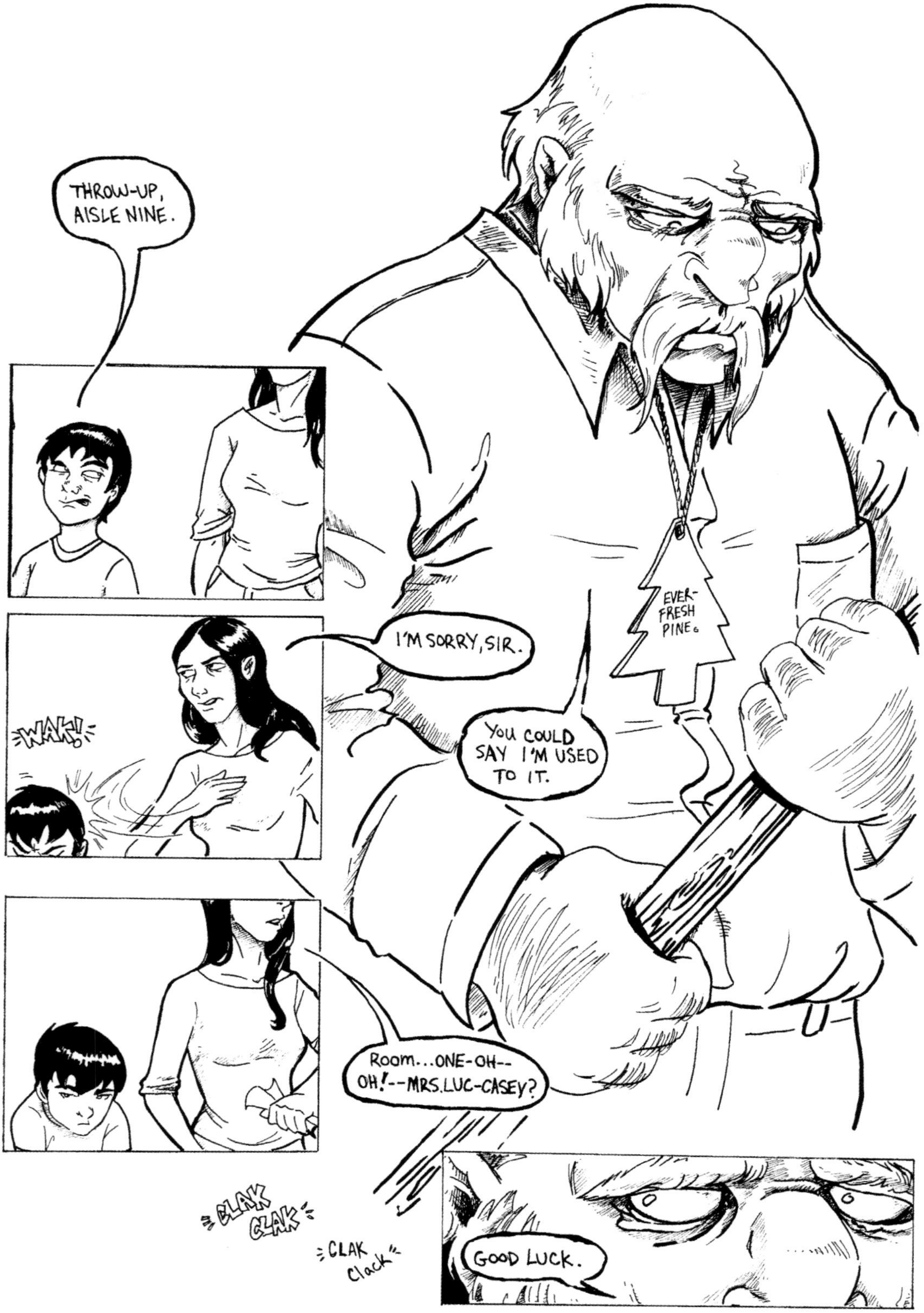
THROW-UP, AISLE NINE.
WAK!
I'M SORRY, SIR.
YOU COULD SAY I'M USED TO IT.
EVER-FRESH PINE
Room...ONE-OH--OH!--MRS.LUC-CASEY?
BLAK CLAK
CLAK Clack
GOOD LUCK.

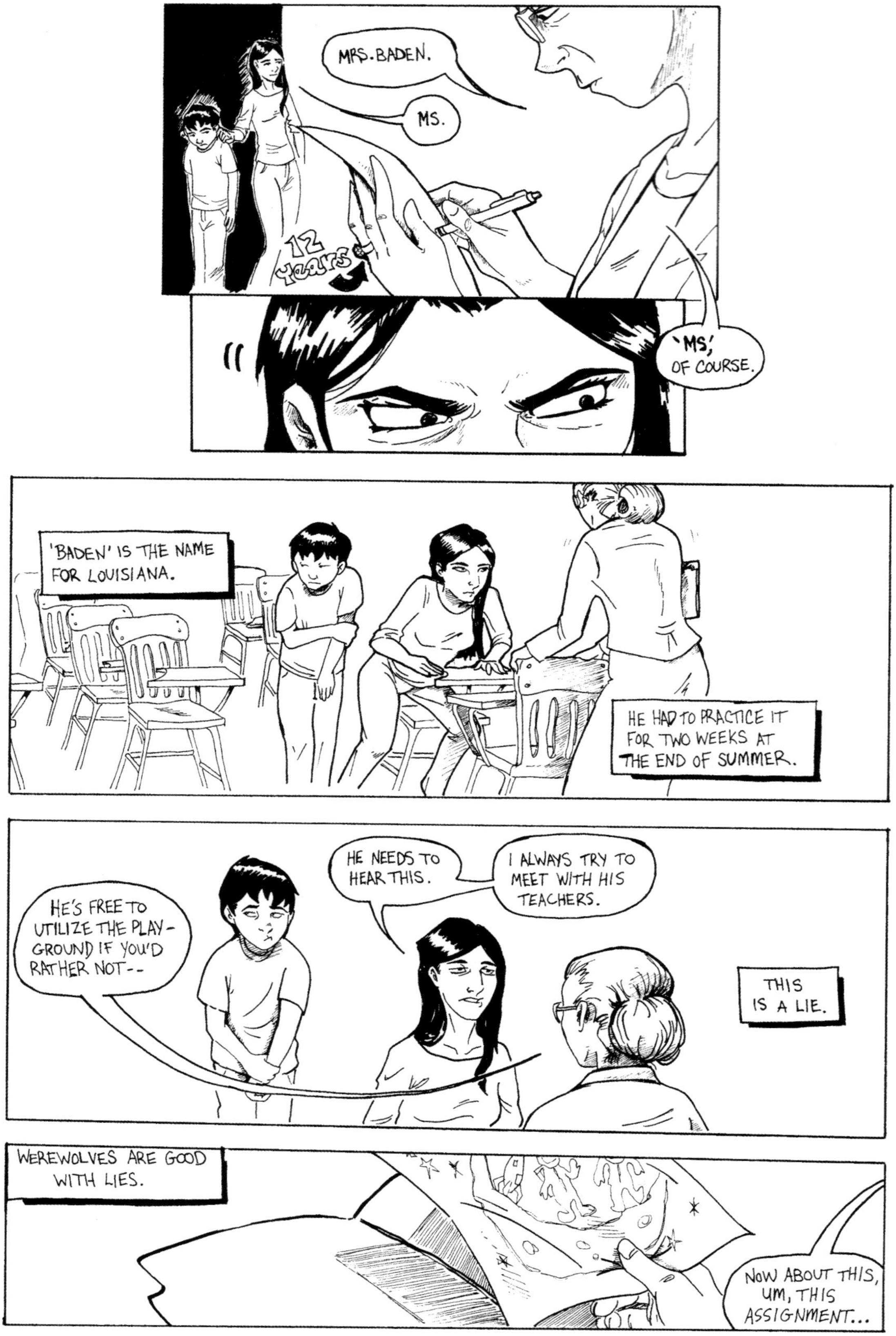
MRS. BADEN.
MS.
12 years
'MS,' OF COURSE.
'BADEN' IS THE NAME FOR LOUISIANA.
HE HAD TO PRACTICE IT FOR TWO WEEKS AT THE END OF SUMMER.
HE'S FREE TO UTILIZE THE PLAY-GROUND IF YOU'D RATHER NOT--
HE NEEDS TO HEAR THIS.
I ALWAYS TRY TO MEET WITH HIS TEACHERS.
THIS IS A LIE.
WEREWOLVES ARE GOOD WITH LIES.
NOW ABOUT THIS, UM, THIS ASSIGNMENT...

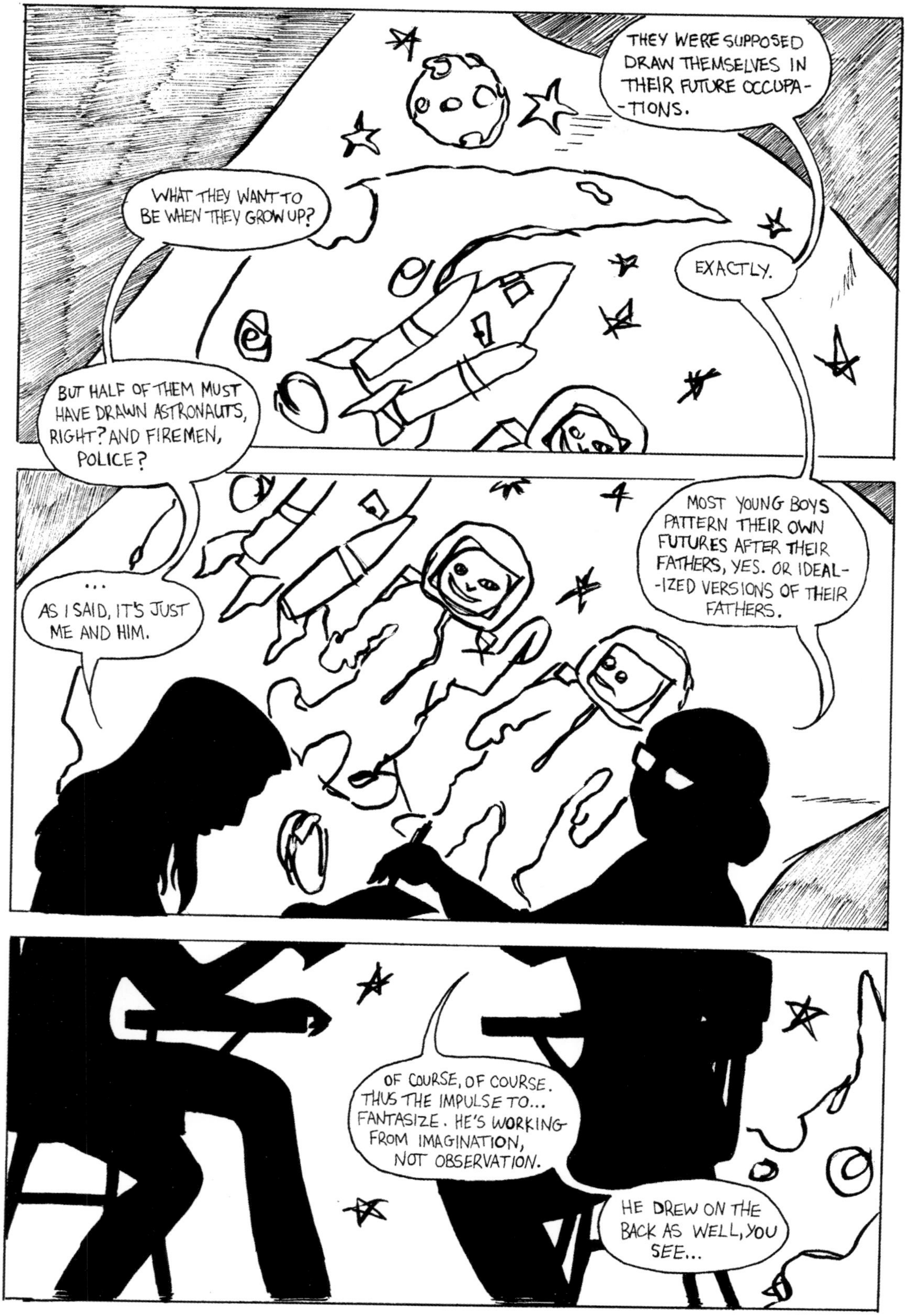
THEY WERE SUPPOSED DRAW THEMSELVES IN THEIR FUTURE OCCUPA- -TIONS.
WHAT THEY WANT TO BE WHEN THEY GROW UP?
EXACTLY.
BUT HALF OF THEM MUST HAVE DRAWN ASTRONAUTS, RIGHT? AND FIREMEN, POLICE?
MOST YOUNG BOYS PATTERN THEIR OWN FUTURES AFTER THEIR FATHERS, YES. OR IDEAL- -IZED VERSIONS OF THEIR FATHERS.
... AS I SAID, IT'S JUST ME AND HIM.
OF COURSE, OF COURSE. THUS THE IMPULSE TO... FANTASIZE. HE'S WORKING FROM IMAGINATION, NOT OBSERVATION.
HE DREW ON THE BACK AS WELL, YOU SEE...

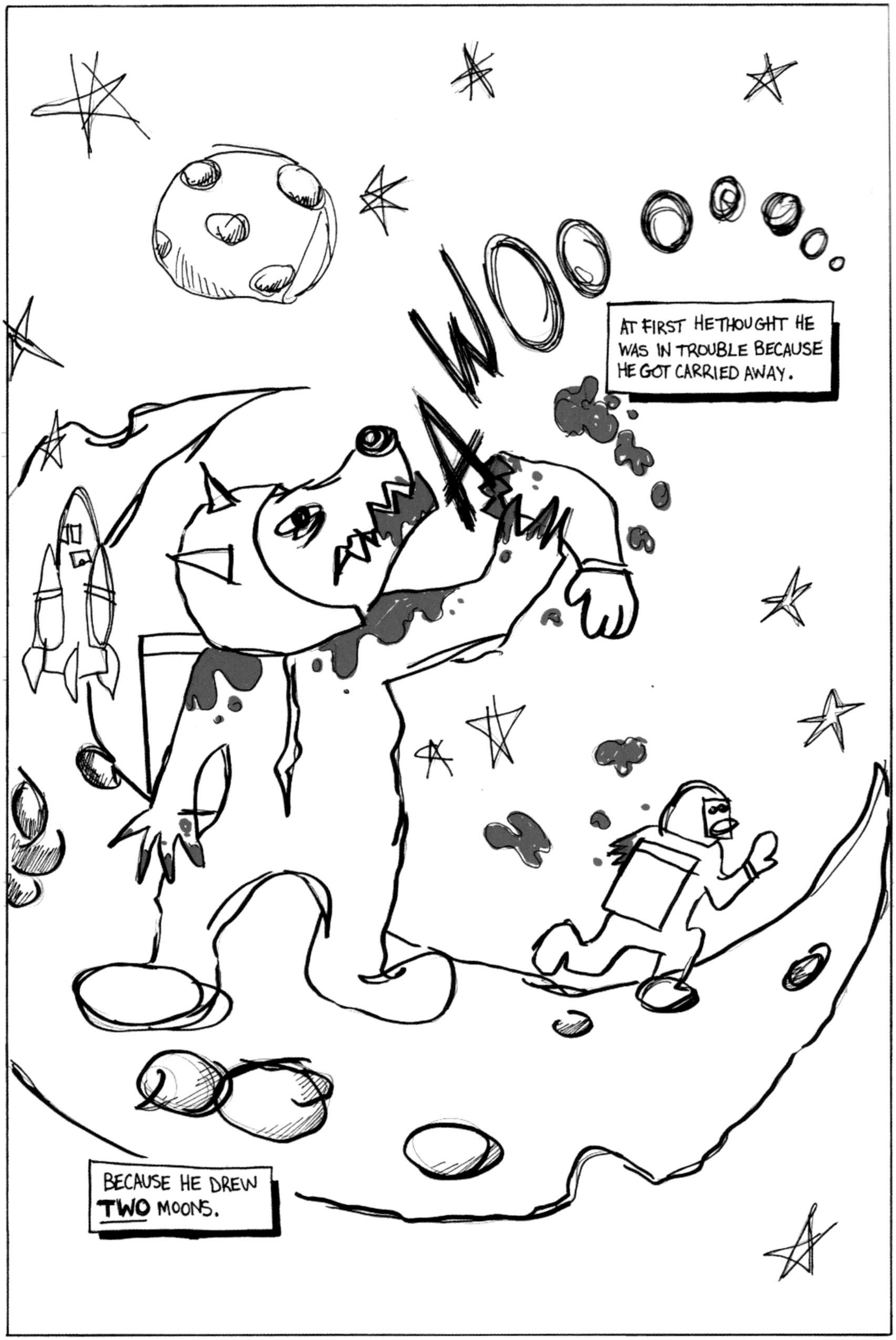
WOOOOOOOO...
AT FIRST HE THOUGHT HE WAS IN TROUBLE BECAUSE HE GOT CARRIED AWAY.
BECAUSE HE DREW TWO MOONS.

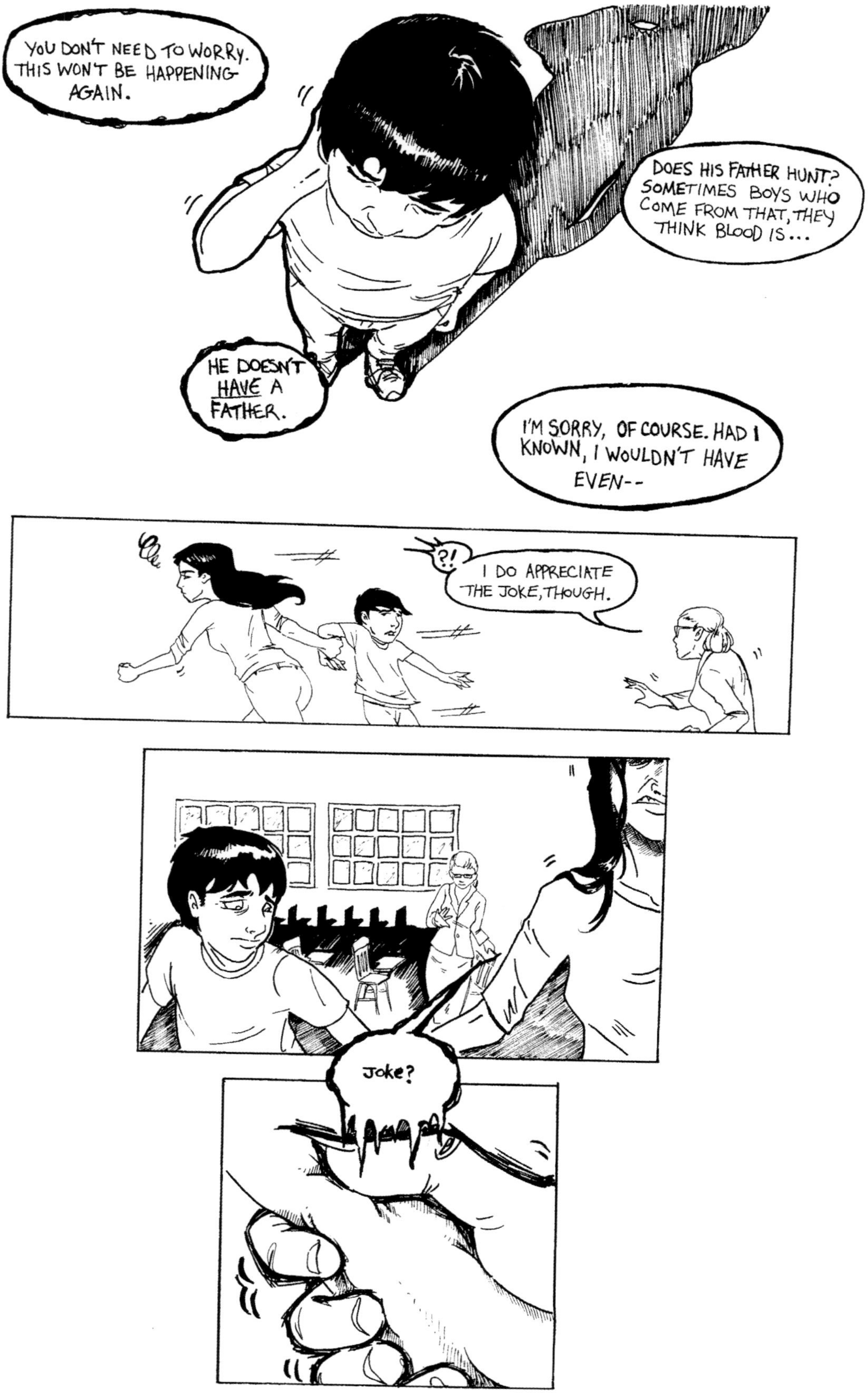
YOU DON'T NEED TO WORRY. THIS WON'T BE HAPPENING AGAIN.
DOES HIS FATHER HUNT? SOMETIMES BOYS WHO COME FROM THAT, THEY THINK BLOOD IS...
HE DOESN'T HAVE A FATHER.
I'M SORRY, OF COURSE. HAD I KNOWN, I WOULDN'T HAVE EVEN--
?!
I DO APPRECIATE THE JOKE, THOUGH.
Joke?

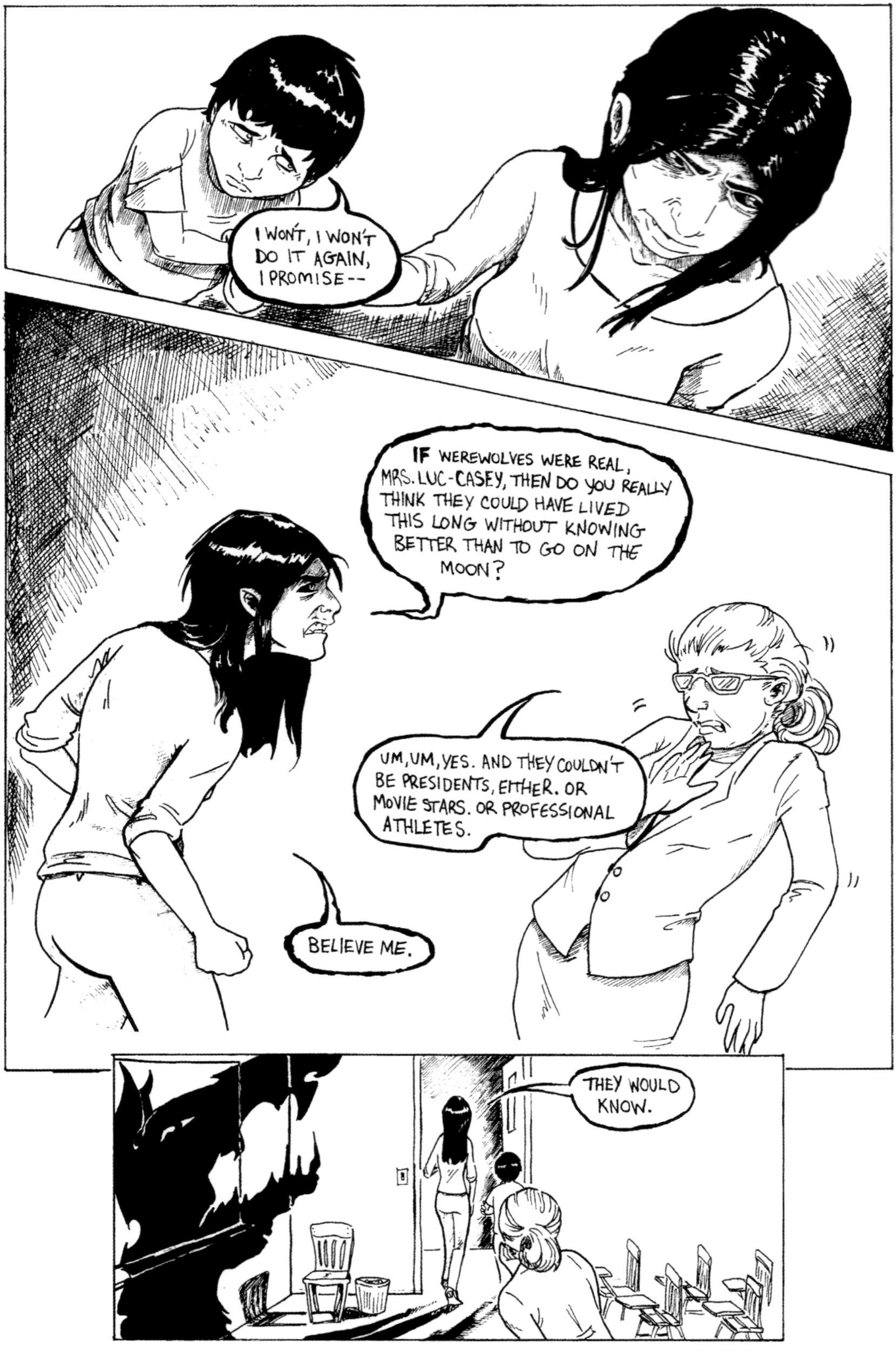
I WON'T, I WON'T DO IT AGAIN, I PROMISE--
IF WEREWOLVES WERE REAL, MRS. LUC-CASEY, THEN DO YOU REALLY THINK THEY COULD HAVE LIVED THIS LONG WITHOUT KNOWING BETTER THAN TO GO ON THE MOON?
UM, UM, YES. AND THEY COULDN'T BE PRESIDENTS, EITHER. OR MOVIE STARS. OR PROFESSIONAL ATHLETES.
BELIEVE ME.
THEY WOULD KNOW.

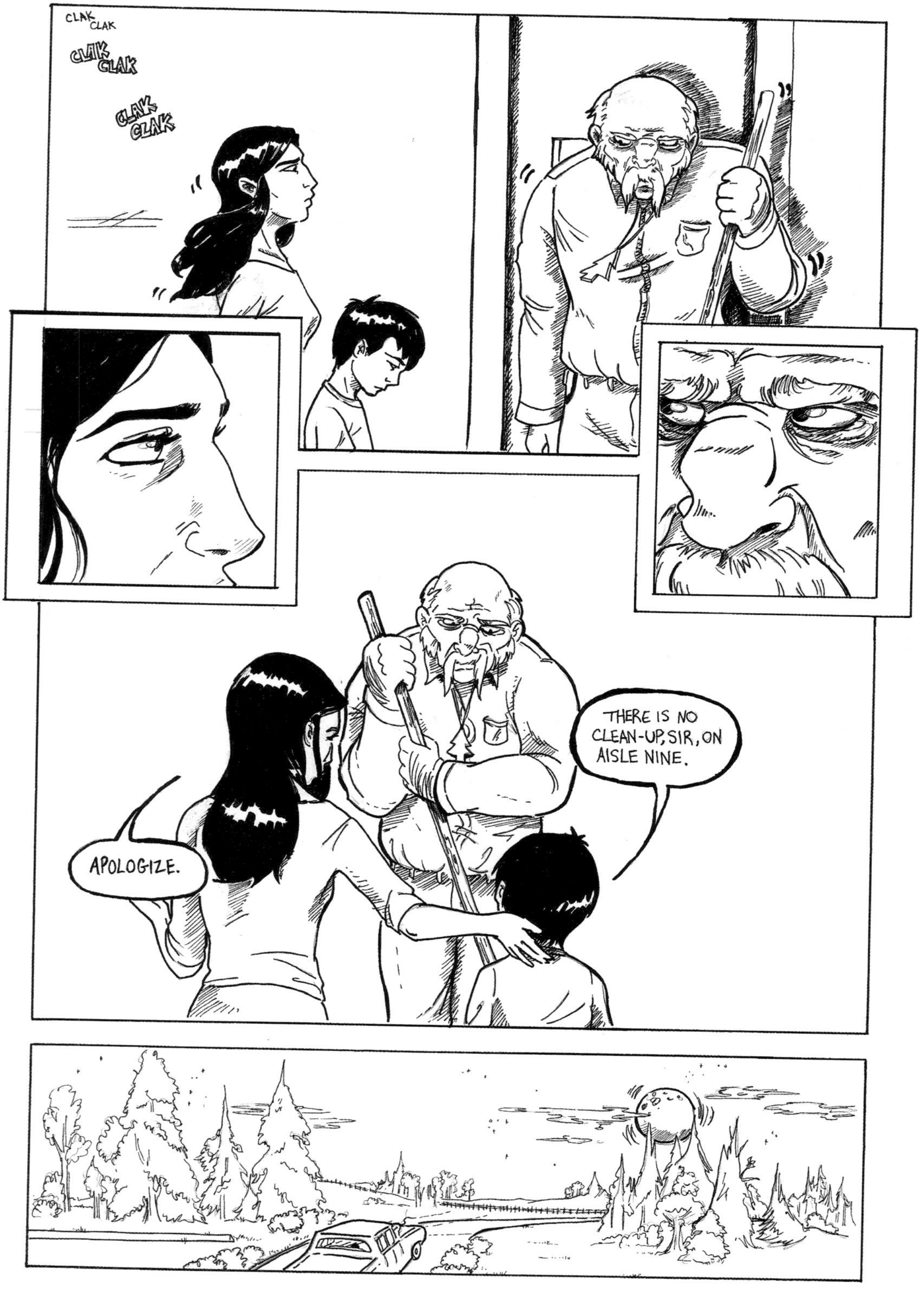
CLAK CLAK
CLAK CLAK
CLAK CLAK
APOLOGIZE.
THERE IS NO CLEAN-UP, SIR, ON AISLE NINE.

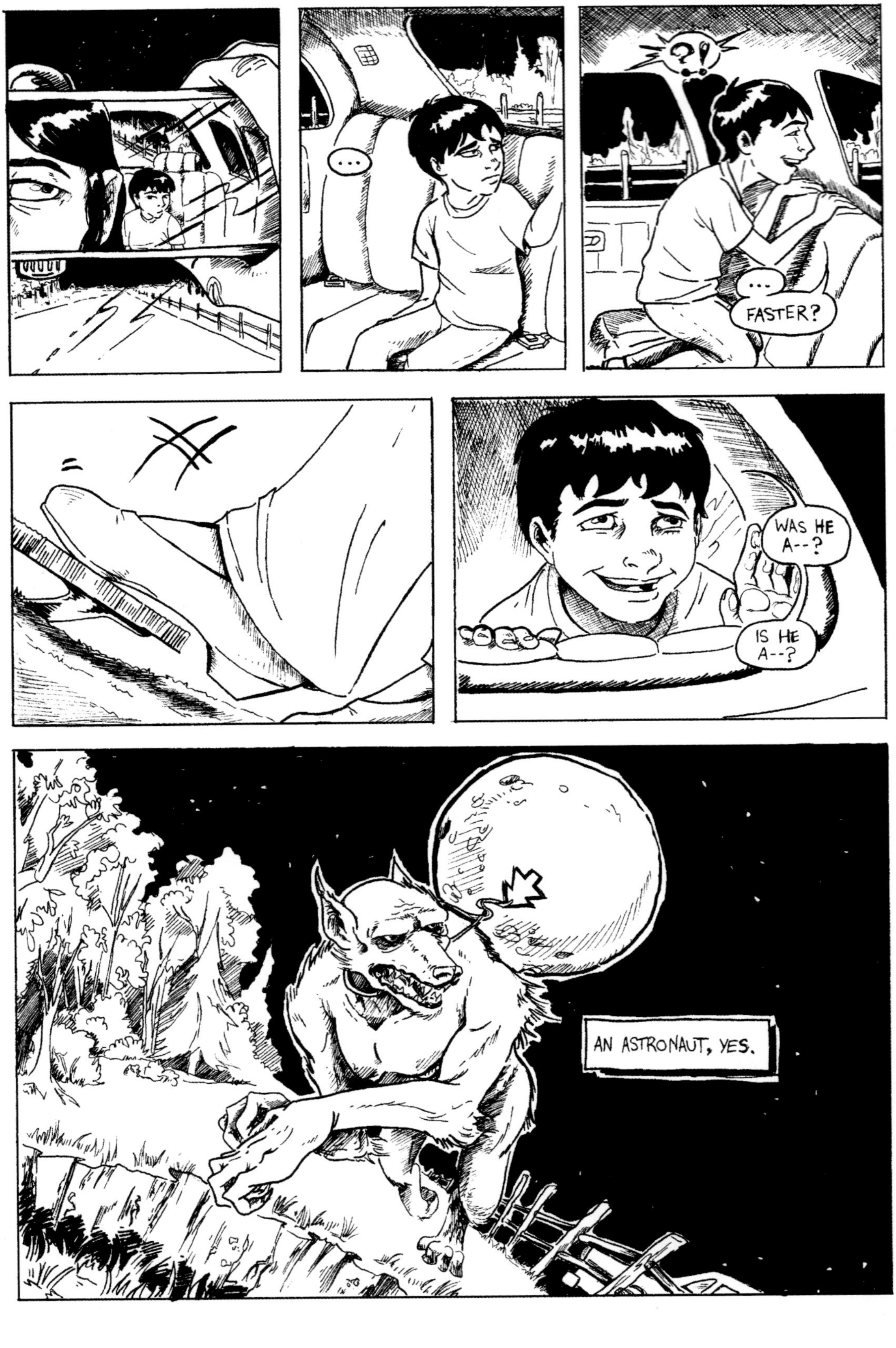
?!
...
...
FASTER?
WAS HE A--?
IS HE A--?
AN ASTRONAUT, YES.

The Prisoner of Haiku

Gordon Henry Jr.

ILLUSTRATION & COLORS: Neal Shannacappo

Gordon Henry Jr. is an enrolled member of the White Earth Anishinaabe Nation in Minnesota. Dr. Henry also is a Professor in the English Department at Michigan State University, where he teaches American Indian Literature, Creative Writing, and courses in the Integrative Arts and Humanities. He serves as Series Editor of the American Indian Studies Series (and the series sub-imprint Makwa Enewed) at Michigan State University Press. Under his editorship the AISS has published research and creative work by an array of scholars, working in a variety of disciplines. Six years ago, while serving as Director of the Native American Institute at Michigan State, he, along with Ellen Cushman, founded the Native American Youth Film Institute. As an offshoot of that project Professor Henry is working with the NAI and the Michigan Inter-Tribal Council, on Indigistory, a community based digital storytelling project. Gordon also is a published poet and fiction writer. In 1995 he received an American Book Award for his novel *The Light People* and his poetry, fiction, and essays have been published extensively, in the United States and Europe. In 2004 he co-published an educational reader on Ojibwe people with George Cornell. In 2007 he published a mixed-genre collection, titled *The Failure of Certain Charms*. He also co-edited a collection of essays on American Indian Literature, titled *Stories through Theories/ Theories through Stories* in 2009. His poetry, fiction, and critical writing has been published extensively internationally. His writing has appeared in journals and anthologies, and in translation in Spain, Greece, Hungary, Italy, the U.K., and Germany. Professor Henry is currently a Gordon Russell Visiting Professor at Dartmouth College, where he is teaching courses in Re-mapping Tribal Narratives and the American Indian Novel.

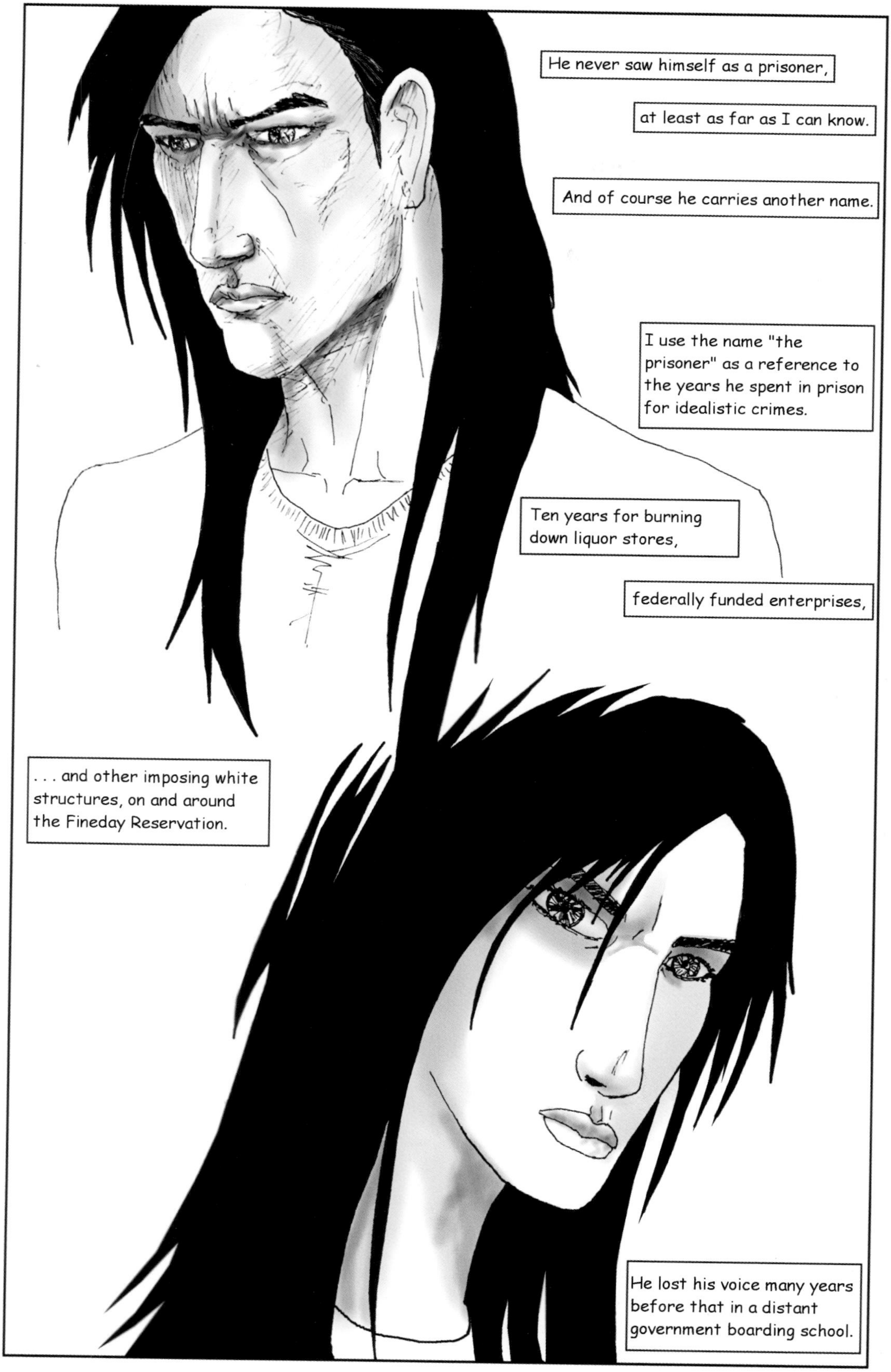
He never saw himself as a prisoner,
at least as far as I can know.
And of course he carries another name.
I use the name "the prisoner" as a reference to the years he spent in prison for idealistic crimes.
Ten years for burning down liquor stores,
federally funded enterprises,
. . . and other imposing white structures, on and around the Fineday Reservation.
He lost his voice many years before that in a distant government boarding school.

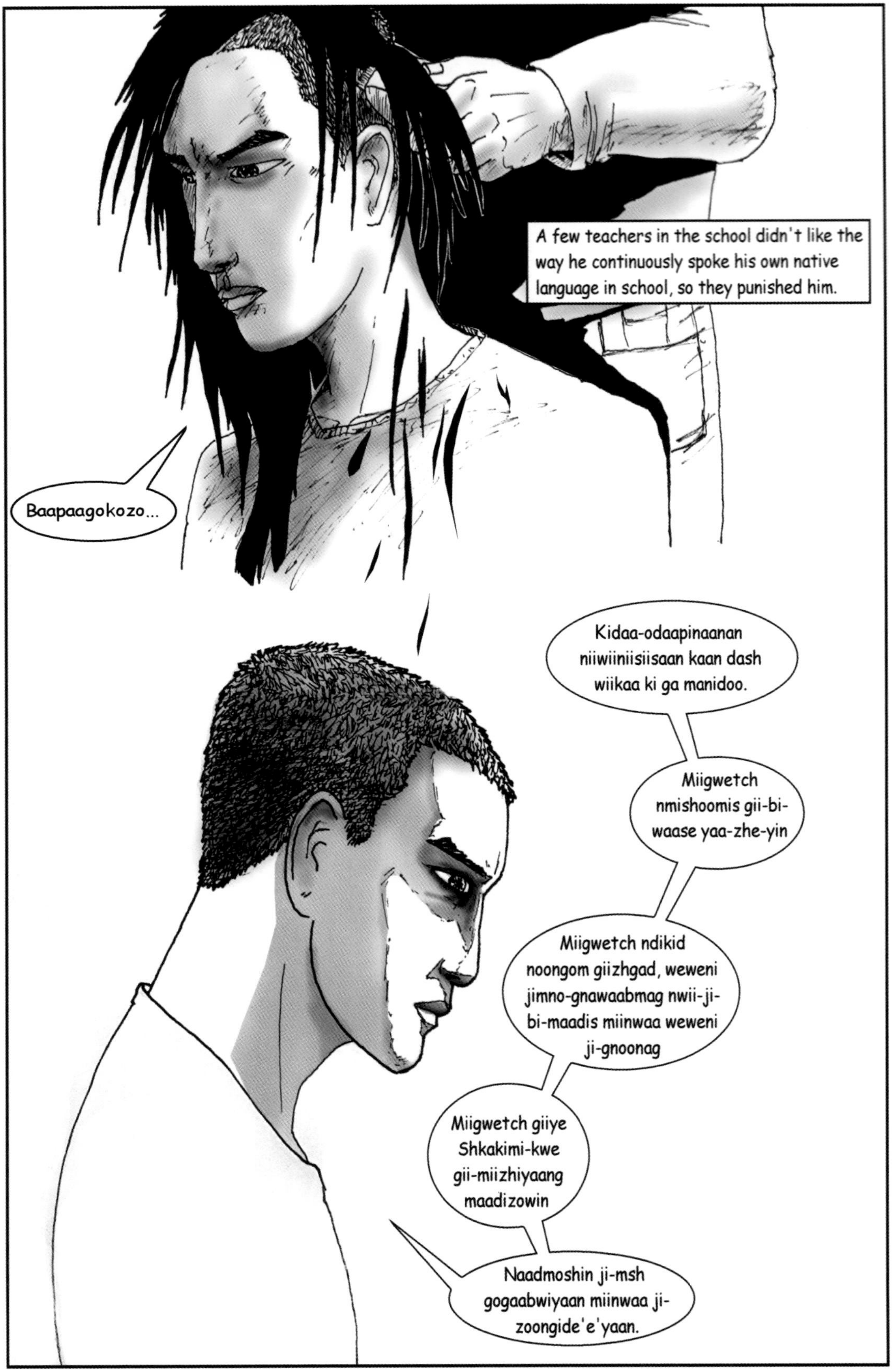
A few teachers in the school didn't like the way he continuously spoke his own native language in school, so they punished him.
Baapaagokozo...
Kidaa-odaapinaanan niiwiiniisiisaan kaan dash wiikaa ki ga manidoo.
Miigwetch nmishoomis gii-bi-waase yaa-zhe-yin
Miigwetch ndikid noongom giizhgad, weweni jimno-gnawaabmag nwii-ji-bi-maadis miinwaa weweni ji-gnoonag
Miigwetch giiye Shkakimi-kwe gii-miizhiyaang maadizowin
Naadmoshin ji-msh gogaabwiyaan miinwaa ji-zoongide'e'yaan.

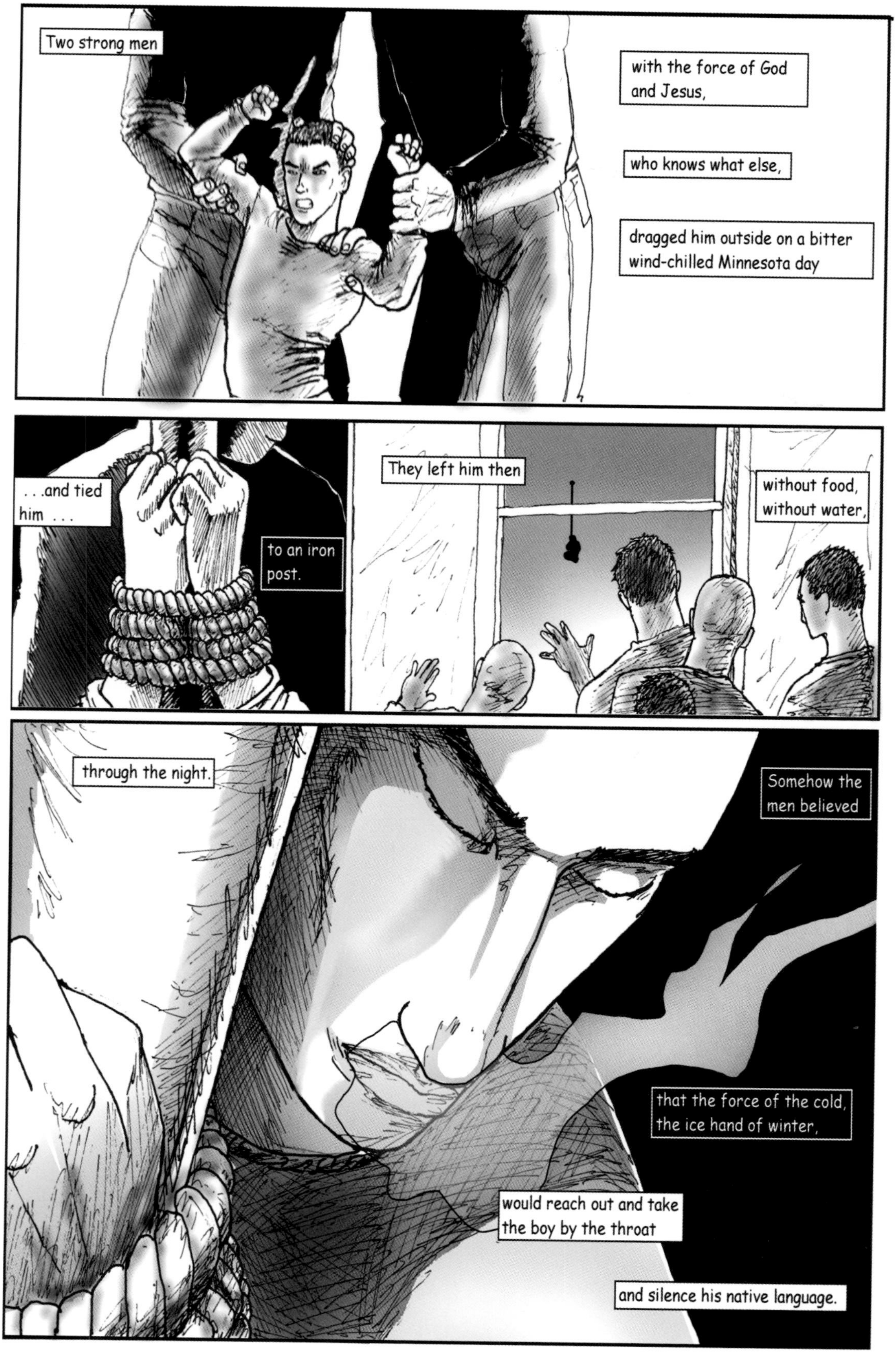
Two strong men
with the force of God and Jesus,
who knows what else,
dragged him outside on a bitter wind-chilled Minnesota day
. . .and tied him . . .
to an iron post.
They left him then
without food, without water,
through the night.
Somehow the men believed
that the force of the cold, the ice hand of winter,
would reach out and take the boy by the throat
and silence his native language.

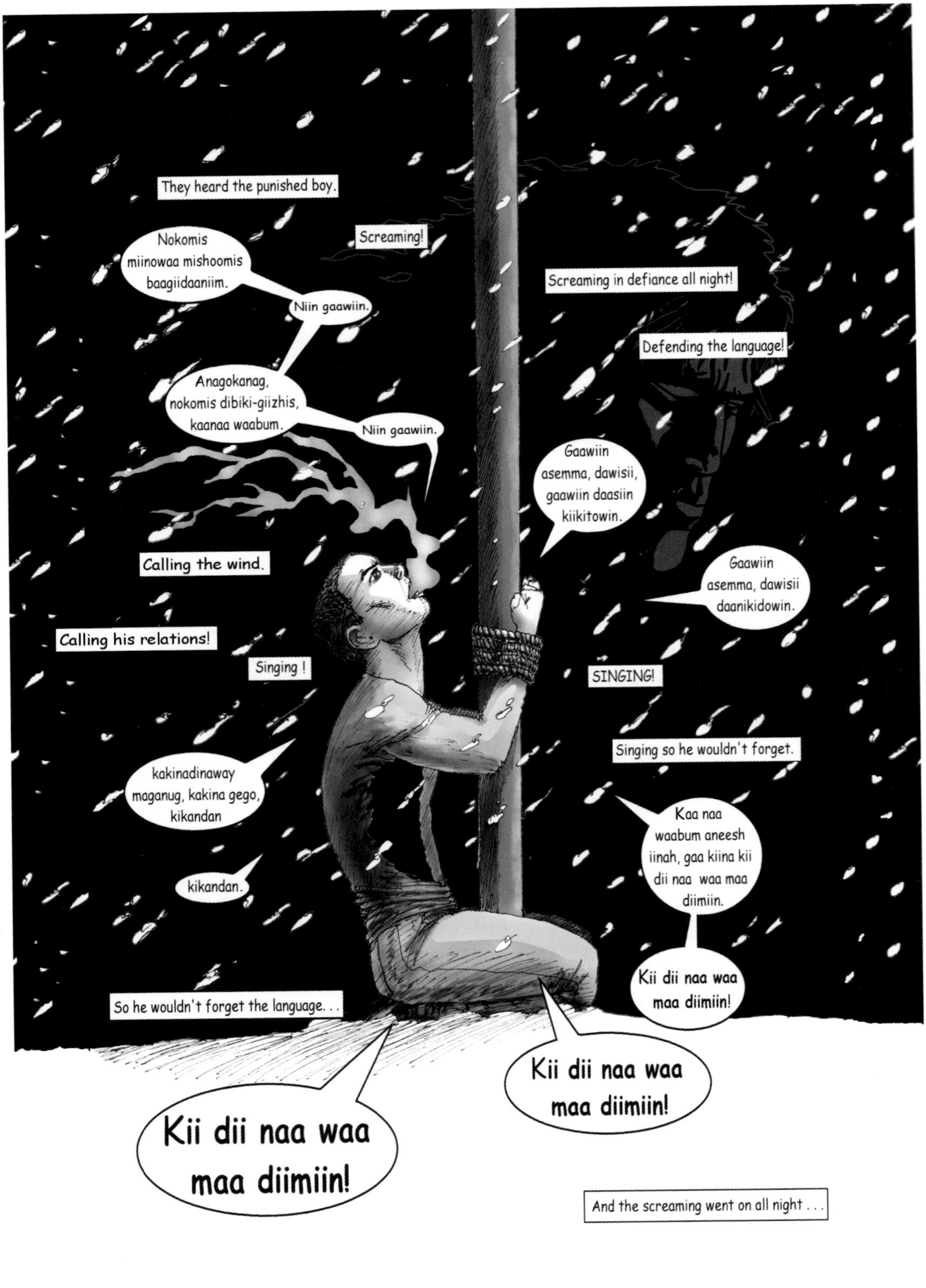
They heard the punished boy.
Screaming!
Nokomis miinowaa mishoomis baagiidaaniim.
Niin gaawiin.
Anagokanag, nokomis dibiki-giizhis, kaanaa waabum.
Niin gaawiin.
Screaming in defiance all night!
Defending the language!
Gaawiin asemma, dawisii, gaawiin daasiin kiikitowin.
Calling the wind.
Gaawiin asemma, dawisii daanikidowin.
Calling his relations!
Singing !
SINGING!
Singing so he wouldn't forget.
kakinadinaway maganug, kakina gego, kikandan
kikandan.
Kaa naa waabum aneesh iinah, gaa kiina kii dii naa waa maa diimiin.
Kii dii naa waa maa diimiin!
So he wouldn't forget the language. . .
Kii dii naa waa maa diimiin!
Kii dii naa waa maa diimiin!
And the screaming went on all night . . .

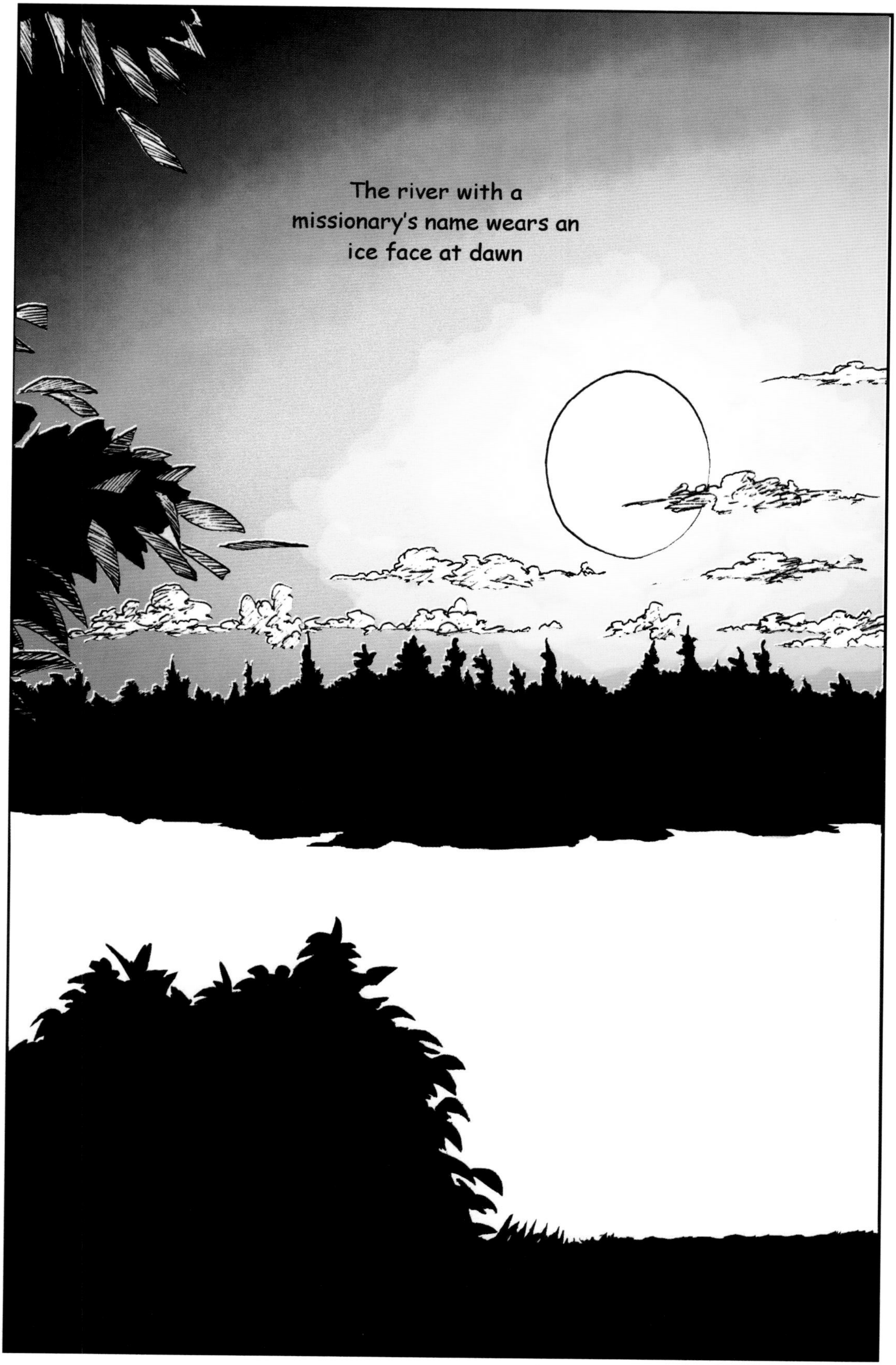
The river with a
missionary's name wears an
ice face at dawn

In the morning on a bright winter day,

when the school fathers went out to untie him . . .

The boy...

Could speak no more

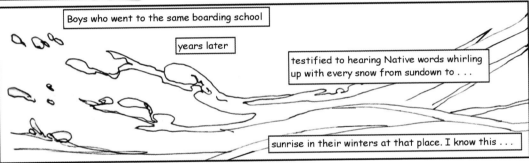

Boys who went to the same boarding school

years later

testified to hearing Native words whirling up with every snow from sundown to . . .

sunrise in their winters at that place. I know this . . .

I slept in the ruins of the boarding school last December,

waiting four nights for snow,

and I heard the voice of the boy.

Unfathomable pain.

Yet the voice

had a strength,

a powerful resilience.

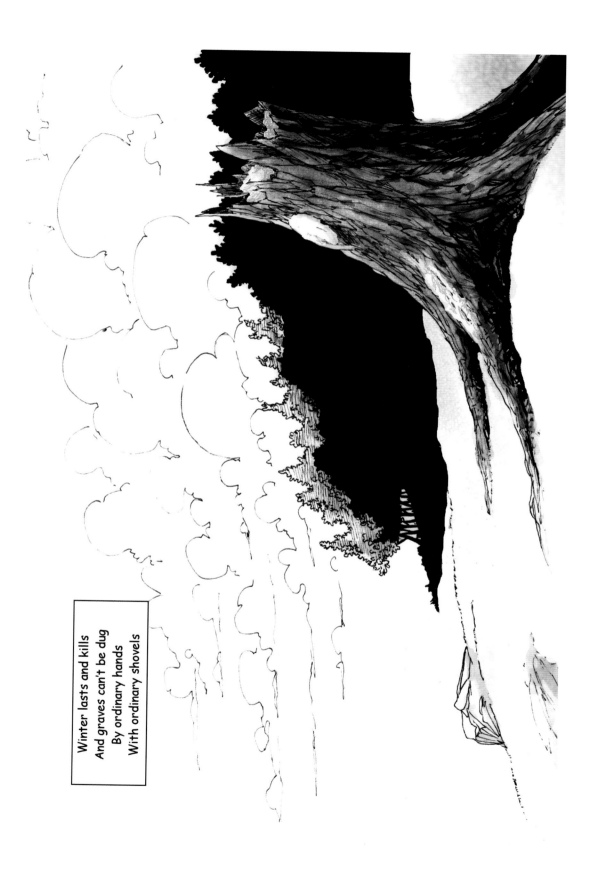

Winter lasts and kills
And graves can't be dug
By ordinary hands
With ordinary shovels

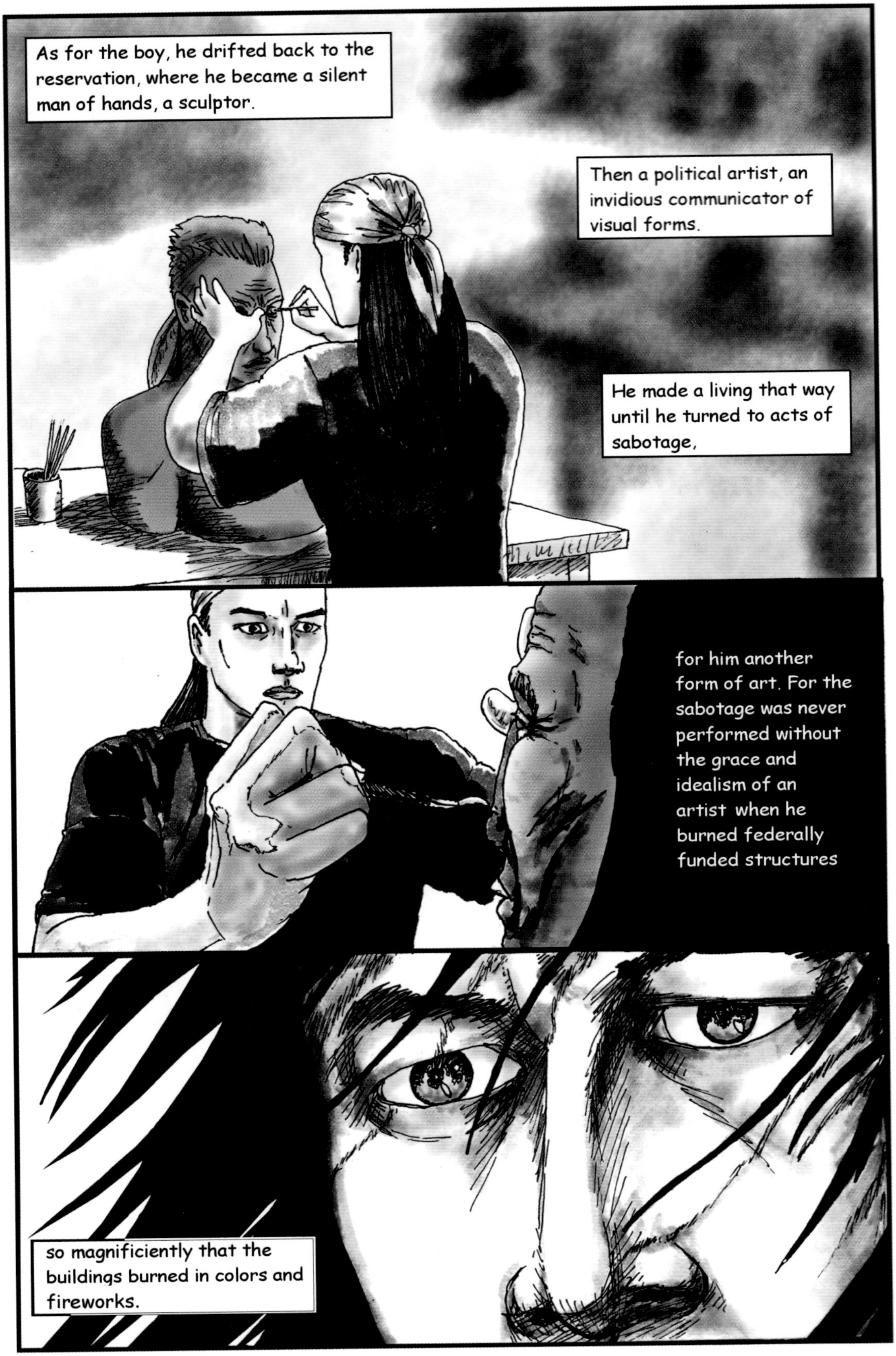
As for the boy, he drifted back to the reservation, where he became a silent man of hands, a sculptor.
Then a political artist, an invidious communicator of visual forms.
He made a living that way until he turned to acts of sabotage,
for him another form of art. For the sabotage was never performed without the grace and idealism of an artist when he burned federally funded structures
so magnificiently that the buildings burned in colors and fireworks.

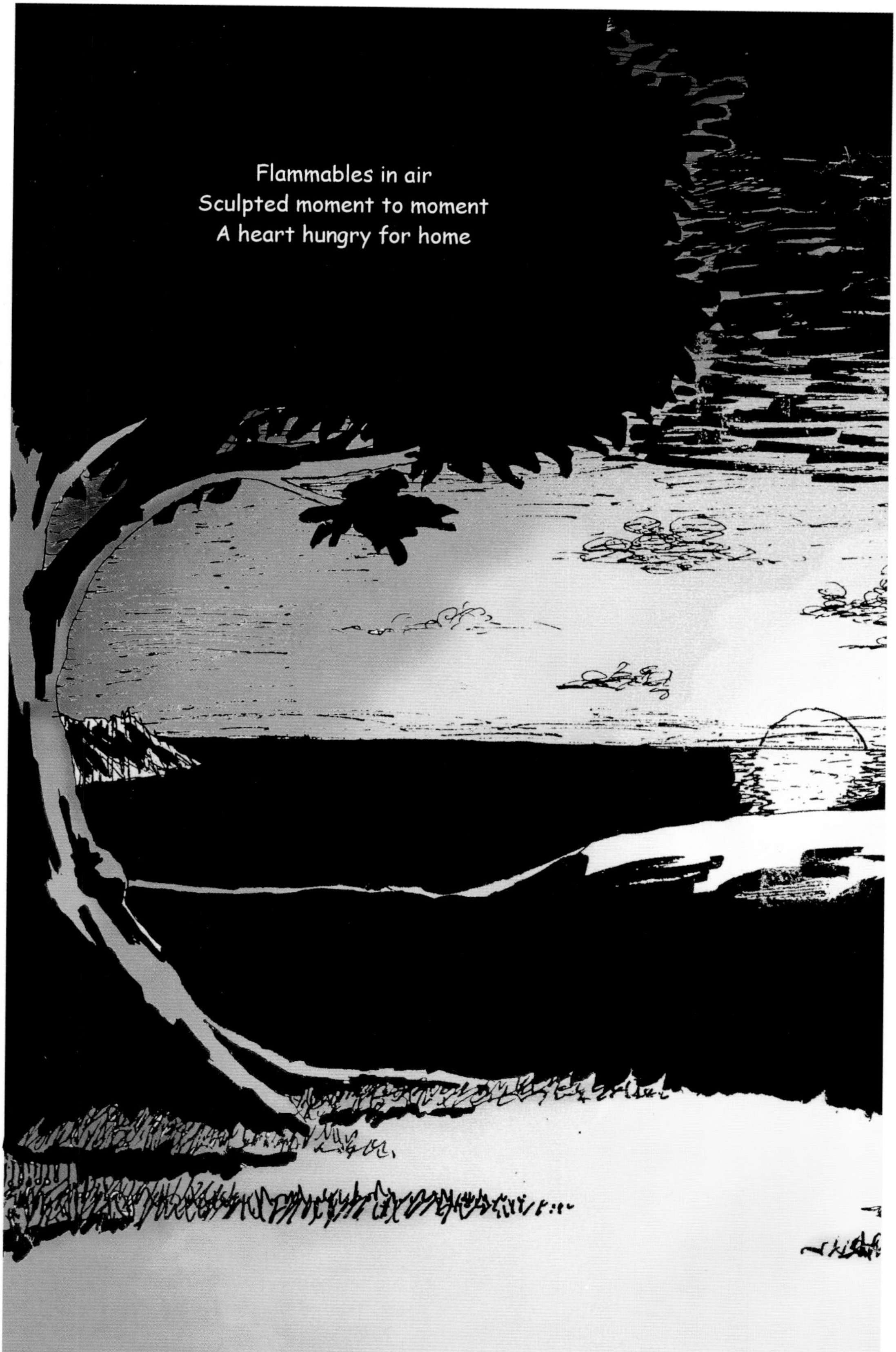
Flammables in air
Sculpted moment to moment
A heart hungry for home

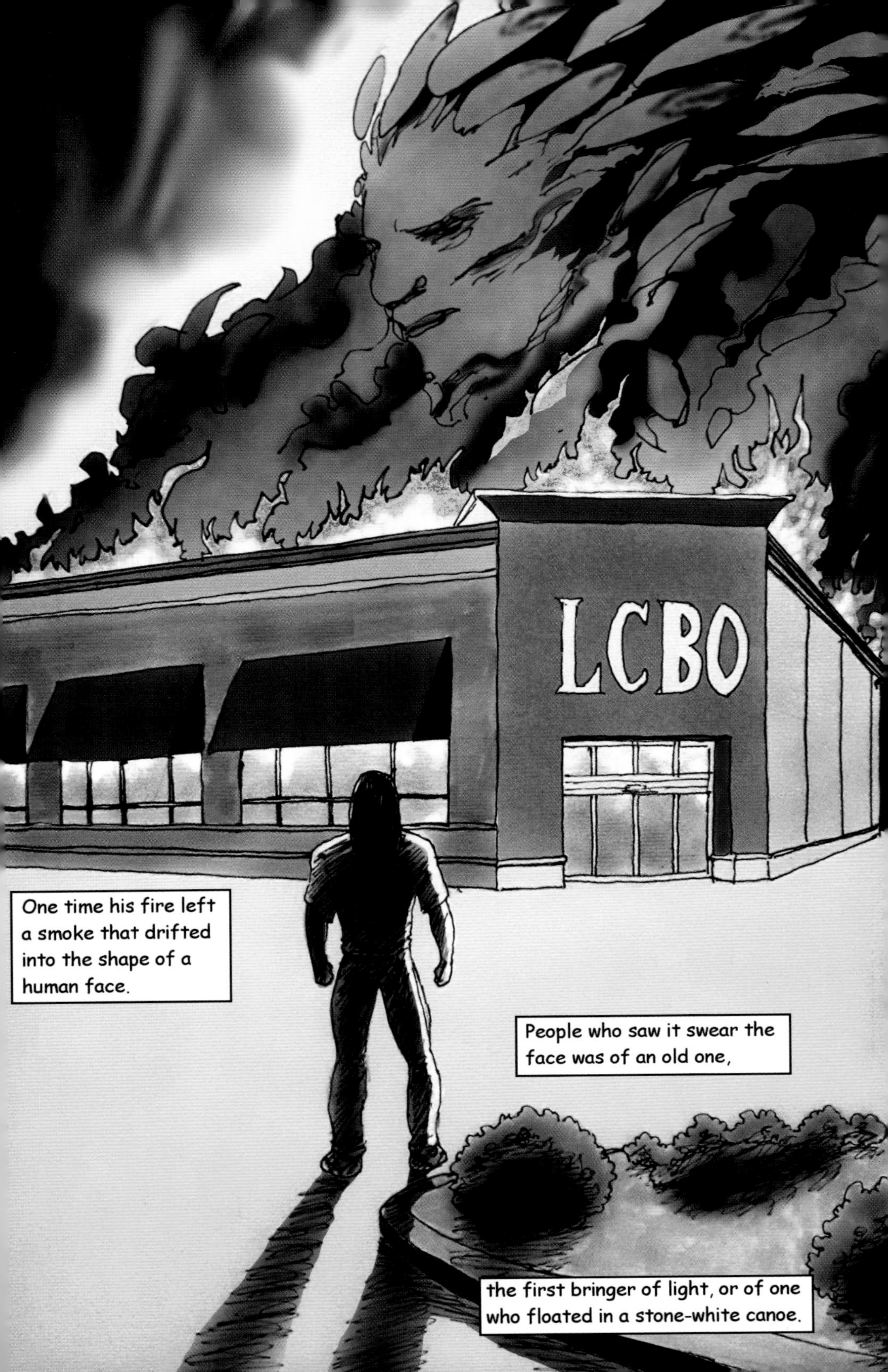
LCBO
One time his fire left a smoke that drifted into the shape of a human face.
People who saw it swear the face was of an old one,
the first bringer of light, or of one who floated in a stone-white canoe.

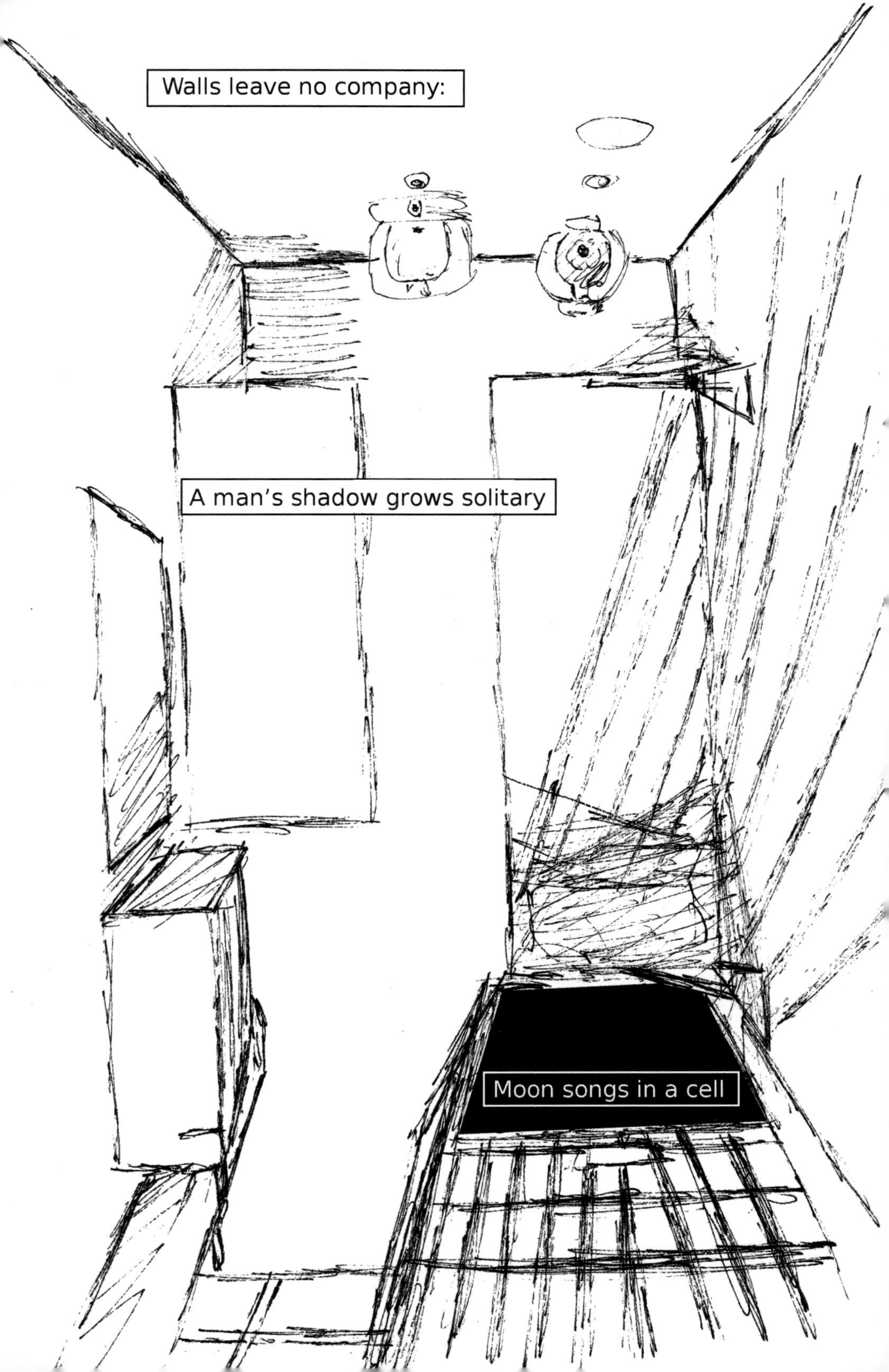
Walls leave no company:
A man's shadow grows solitary
Moon songs in a cell

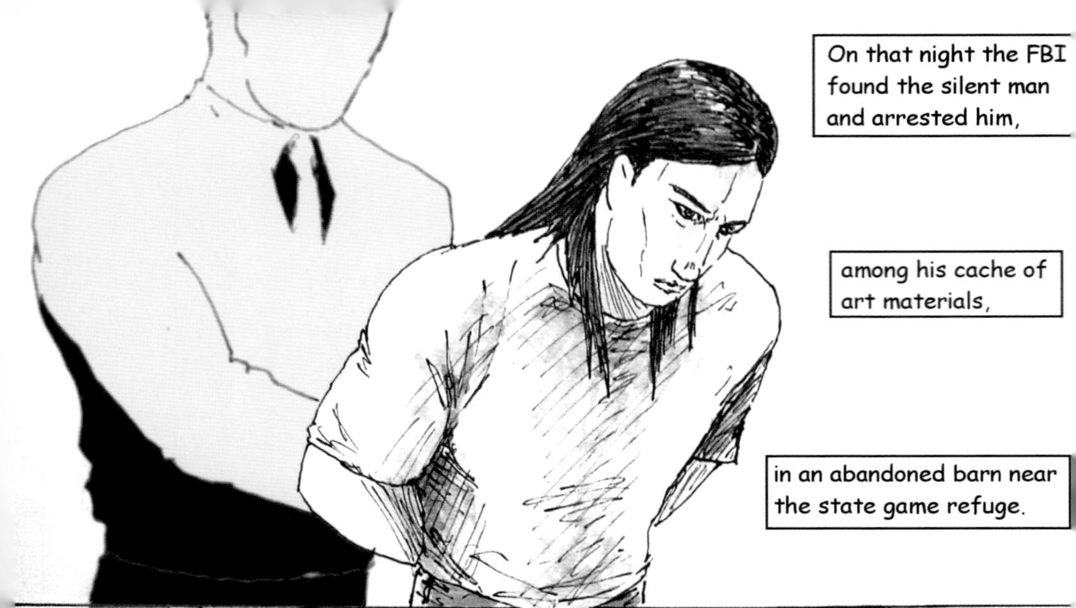
On that night the FBI found the silent man and arrested him,
among his cache of art materials,
in an abandoned barn near the state game refuge.

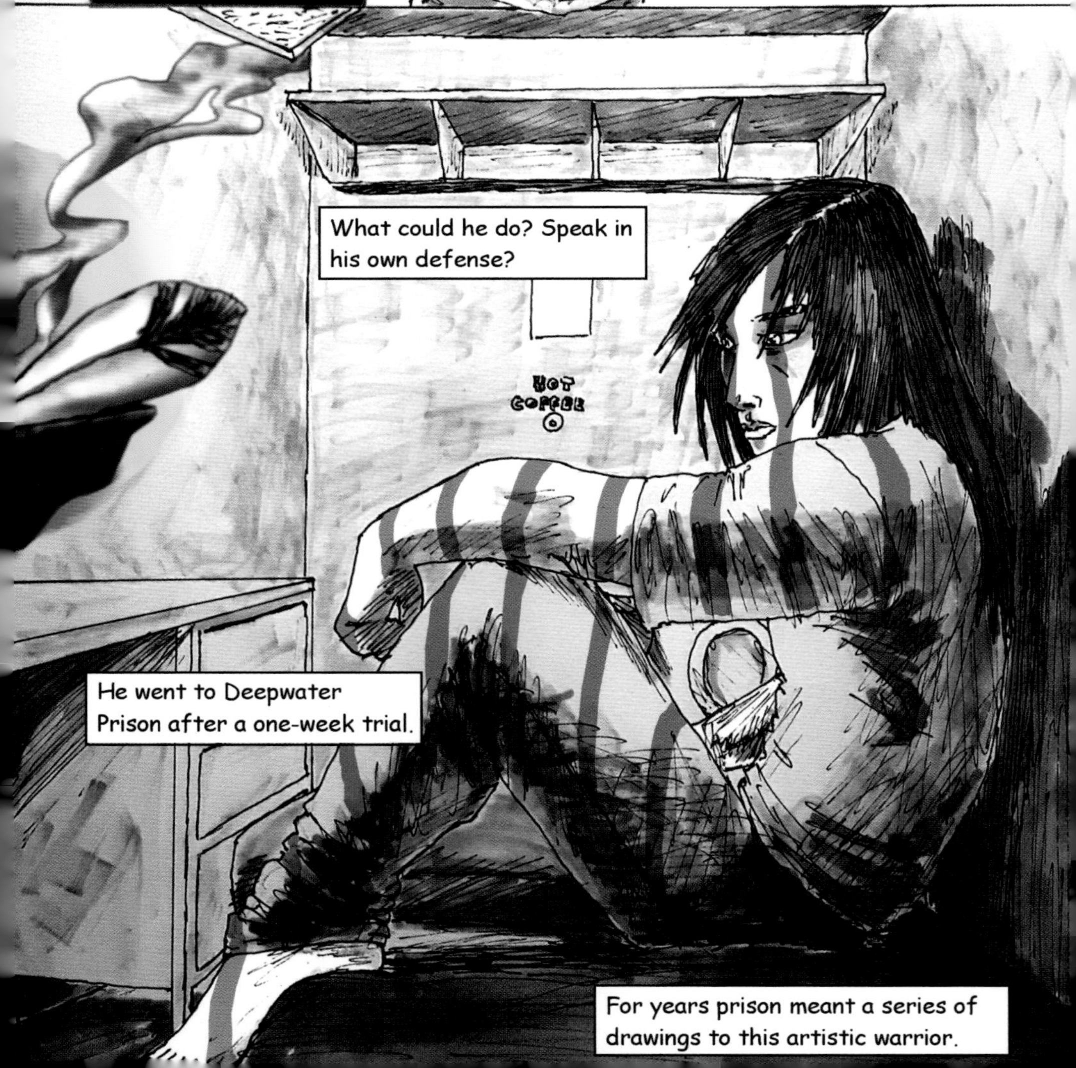
What could he do? Speak in his own defense?
HOT COFFEE
He went to Deepwater Prison after a one-week trial.
For years prison meant a series of drawings to this artistic warrior.

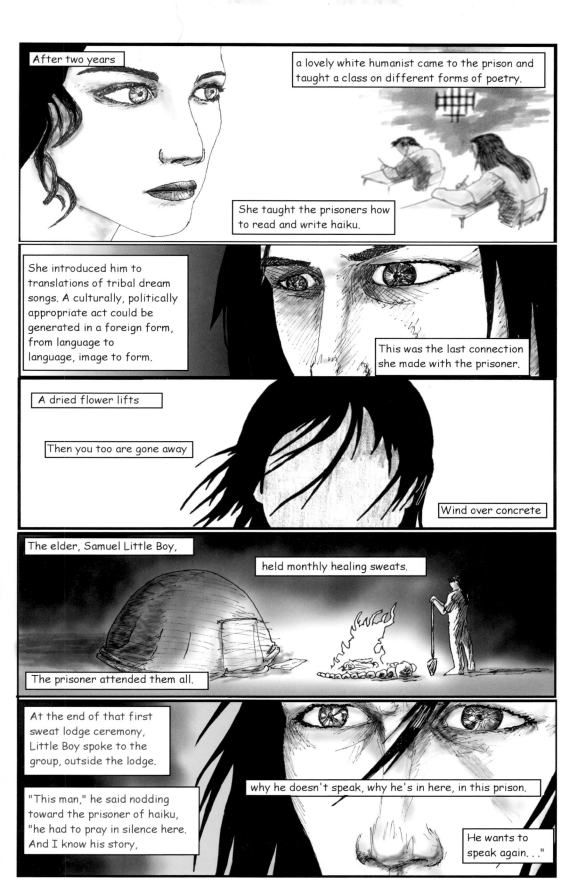

After two years

a lovely white humanist came to the prison and taught a class on different forms of poetry.

She taught the prisoners how to read and write haiku.

She introduced him to translations of tribal dream songs. A culturally, politically appropriate act could be generated in a foreign form, from language to language, image to form.

This was the last connection she made with the prisoner.

A dried flower lifts

Then you too are gone away

Wind over concrete

The elder, Samuel Little Boy,

held monthly healing sweats.

The prisoner attended them all.

At the end of that first sweat lodge ceremony, Little Boy spoke to the group, outside the lodge.

"This man," he said nodding toward the prisoner of haiku, "he had to pray in silence here. And I know his story,

why he doesn't speak, why he's in here, in this prison.

He wants to speak again. . ."

29

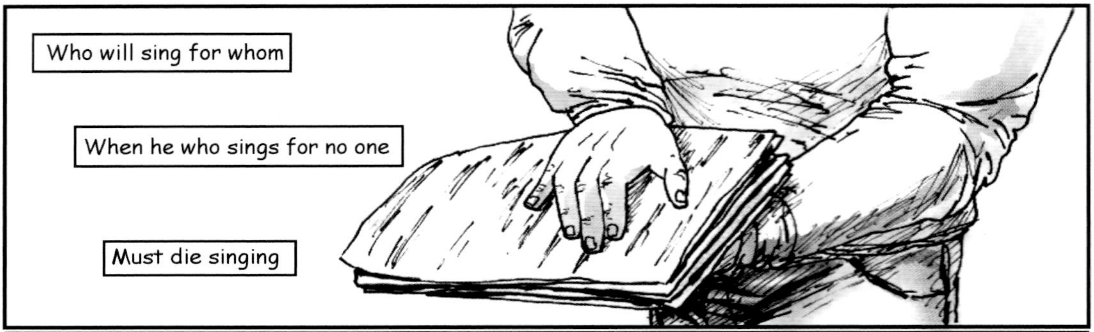
Who will sing for whom
When he who sings for no one
Must die singing

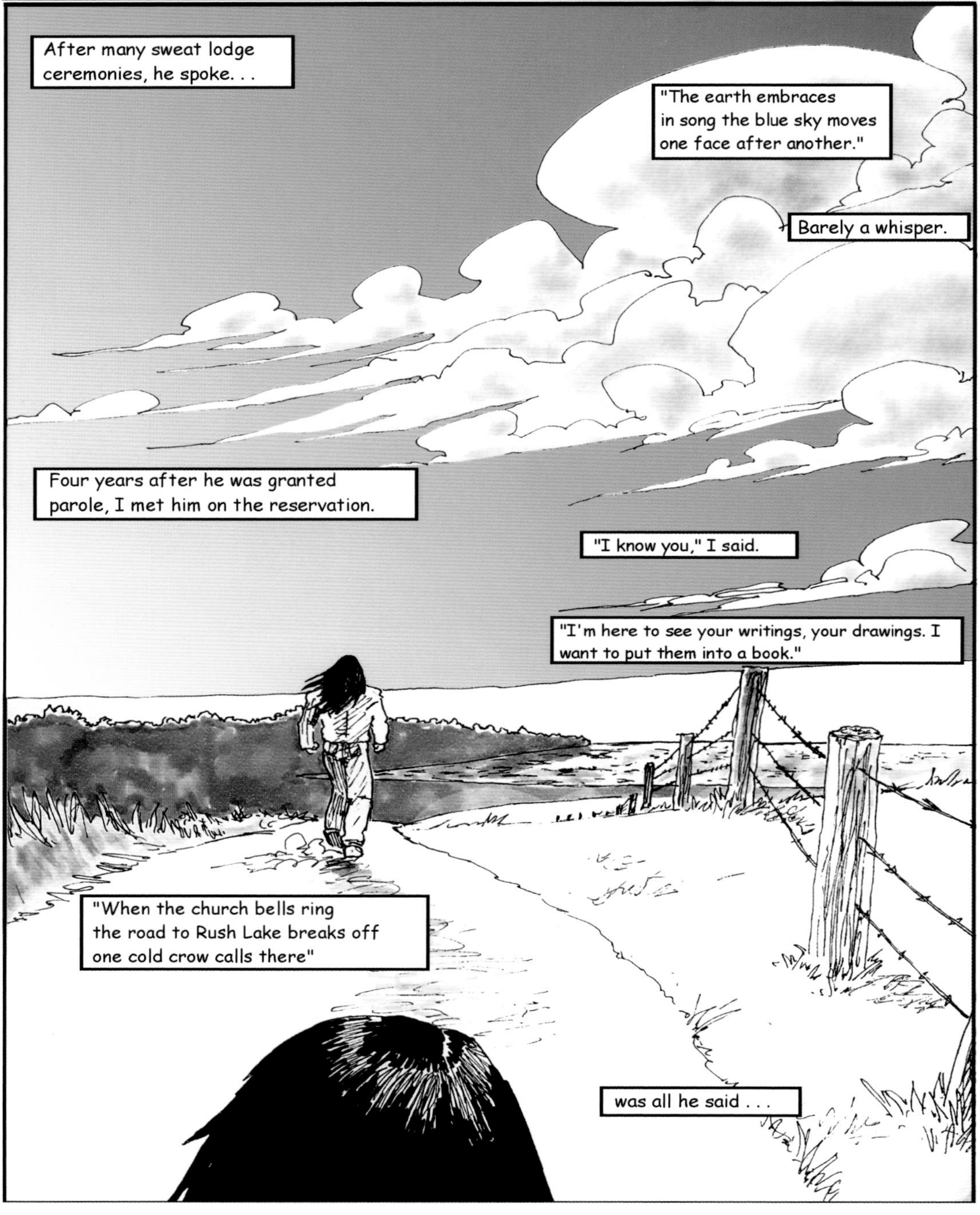
After many sweat lodge ceremonies, he spoke. . .
"The earth embraces in song the blue sky moves one face after another."
Barely a whisper.
Four years after he was granted parole, I met him on the reservation.
"I know you," I said.
"I'm here to see your writings, your drawings. I want to put them into a book."
"When the church bells ring the road to Rush Lake breaks off one cold crow calls there"
was all he said . . .

Ice Tricksters

Gerald Vizenor

ILLUSTRATION & COLORS: GMB Chomichuk

Gerald Vizenor is Professor of American Studies at the University of New Mexico, and Professor Emeritus at the University of California, Berkeley. He was born in Minneapolis in 1934. He is an enrolled member of the Minnesota Chippewa Tribe, White Earth Reservation. Vizenor attended New York University for one year, transferring to the University of Minnesota where he earned his BA in 1960. His graduate studies include University of Minnesota and Harvard University. His career includes work for the Minnesota Department of Corrections and the *Minneapolis Tribune*. Vizenor's teaching career includes professorships at Lake Forest College, Bemidji State University, University of Minnesota, University of Oklahoma, University of California, Berkeley, and University of California, Santa Cruz, where he was provost of Kresge College as well as professor of literature and American Studies. He is the author of *Chasers*, *Griever*, and *Interior Landscapes.*

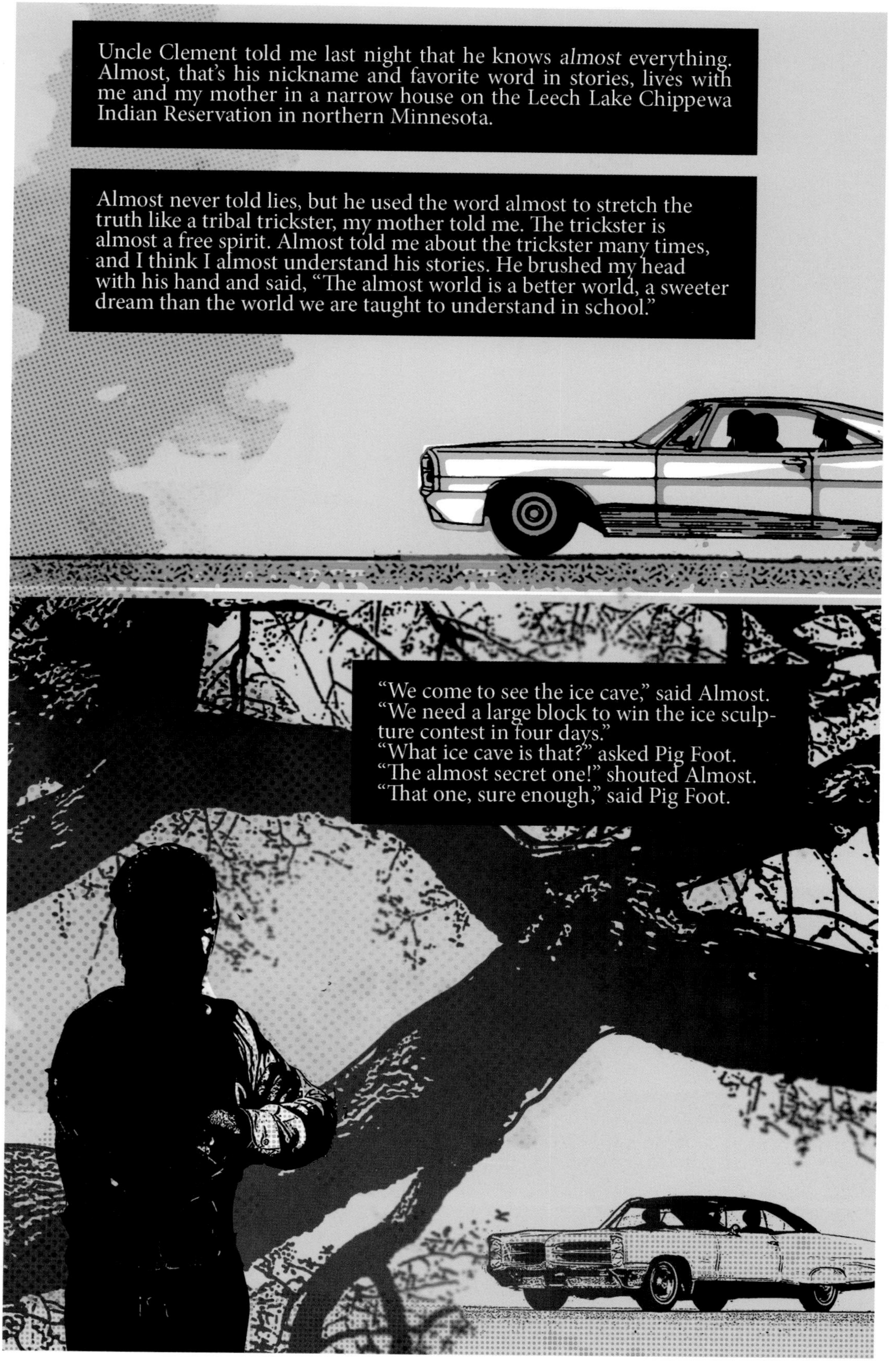
Uncle Clement told me last night that he knows *almost* everything. Almost, that's his nickname and favorite word in stories, lives with me and my mother in a narrow house on the Leech Lake Chippewa Indian Reservation in northern Minnesota.
Almost never told lies, but he used the word almost to stretch the truth like a tribal trickster, my mother told me. The trickster is almost a free spirit. Almost told me about the trickster many times, and I think I almost understand his stories. He brushed my head with his hand and said, "The almost world is a better world, a sweeter dream than the world we are taught to understand in school."
"We come to see the ice cave," said Almost. "We need a large block to win the ice sculpture contest in four days."
"What ice cave is that?" asked Pig Foot.
"The almost secret one!" shouted Almost.
"That one, sure enough," said Pig Foot.

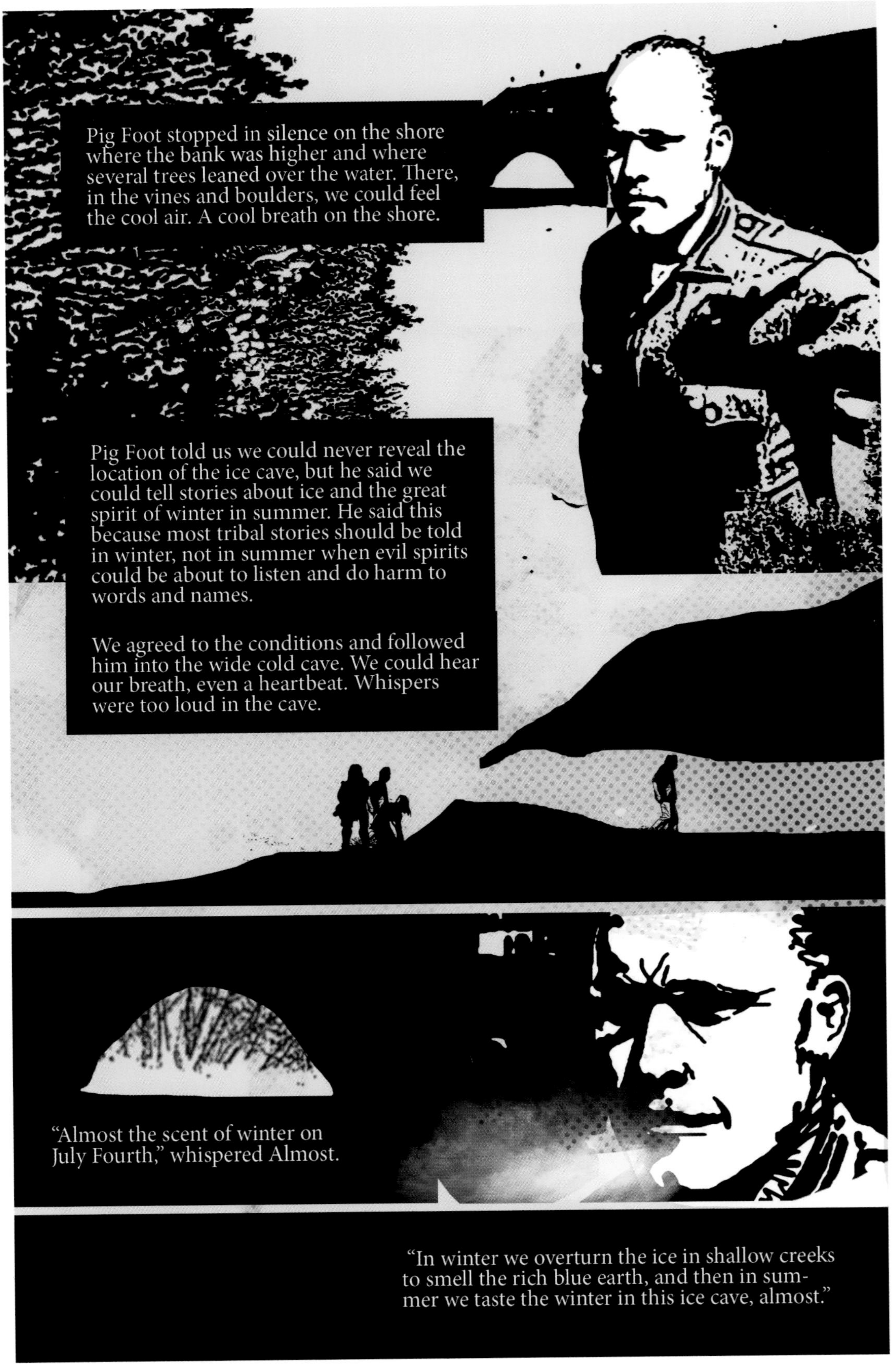

Pig Foot stopped in silence on the shore where the bank was higher and where several trees leaned over the water. There, in the vines and boulders, we could feel the cool air. A cool breath on the shore.
Pig Foot told us we could never reveal the location of the ice cave, but he said we could tell stories about ice and the great spirit of winter in summer. He said this because most tribal stories should be told in winter, not in summer when evil spirits could be about to listen and do harm to words and names.
We agreed to the conditions and followed him into the wide cold cave. We could hear our breath, even a heartbeat. Whispers were too loud in the cave.
"Almost the scent of winter on July Fourth," whispered Almost.
"In winter we overturn the ice in shallow creeks to smell the rich blue earth, and then in summer we taste the winter in this ice cave, almost."

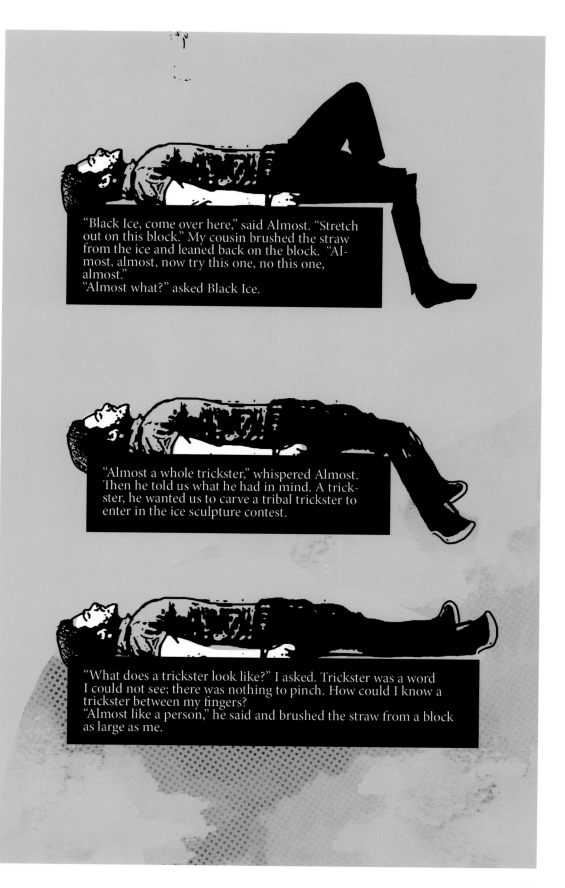

"Black Ice, come over here," said Almost. "Stretch out on this block." My cousin brushed the straw from the ice and leaned back on the block. "Almost, almost, now try this one, no this one, almost."
"Almost what?" asked Black Ice.

"Almost a whole trickster," whispered Almost. Then he told us what he had in mind. A trickster, he wanted us to carve a tribal trickster to enter in the ice sculpture contest.

"What does a trickster look like?" I asked. Trickster was a word I could not see; there was nothing to pinch. How could I know a trickster between my fingers?
"Almost like a person," he said and brushed the straw from a block as large as me.

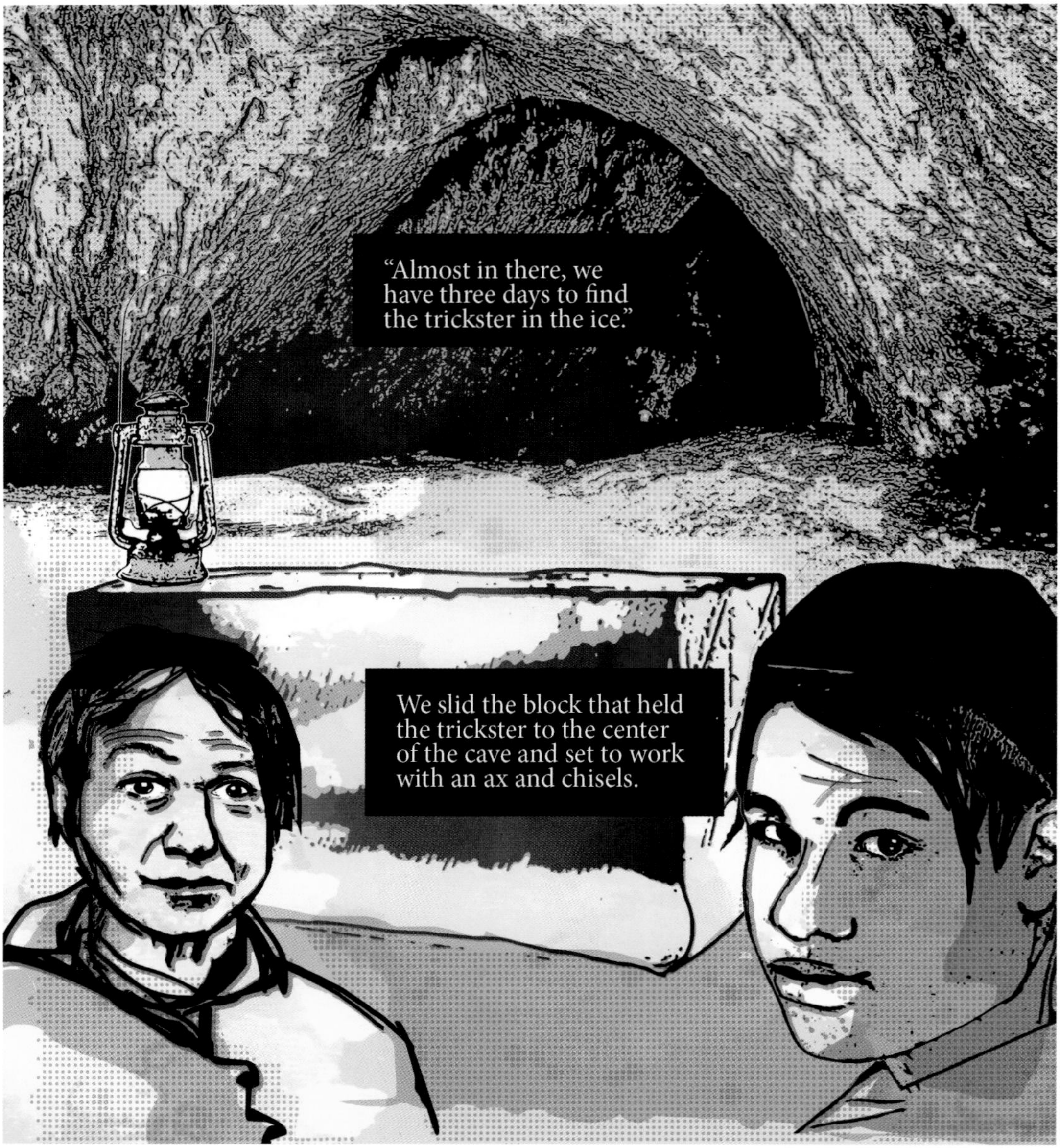
"Almost in there, we have three days to find the trickster in the ice."
We slid the block that held the trickster to the center of the cave and set to work with an ax and chisels.

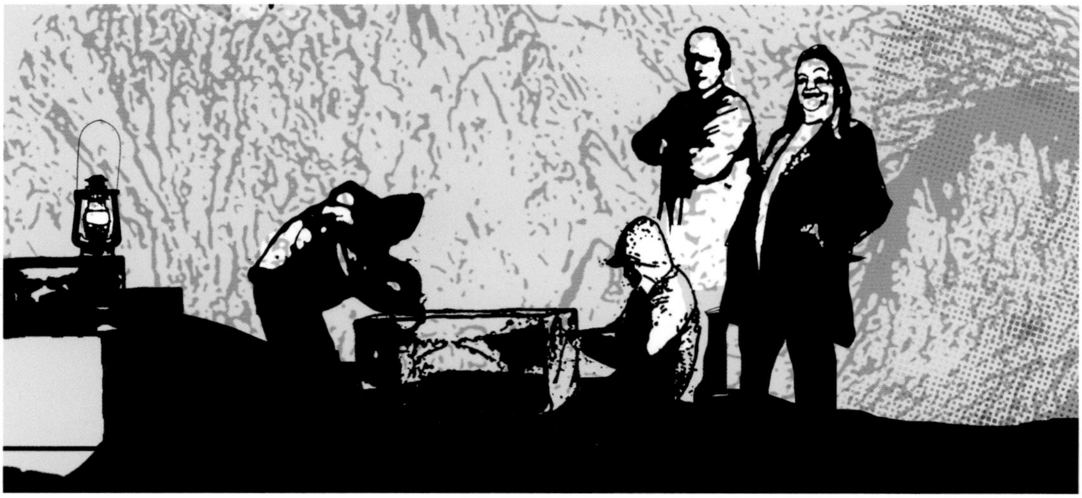

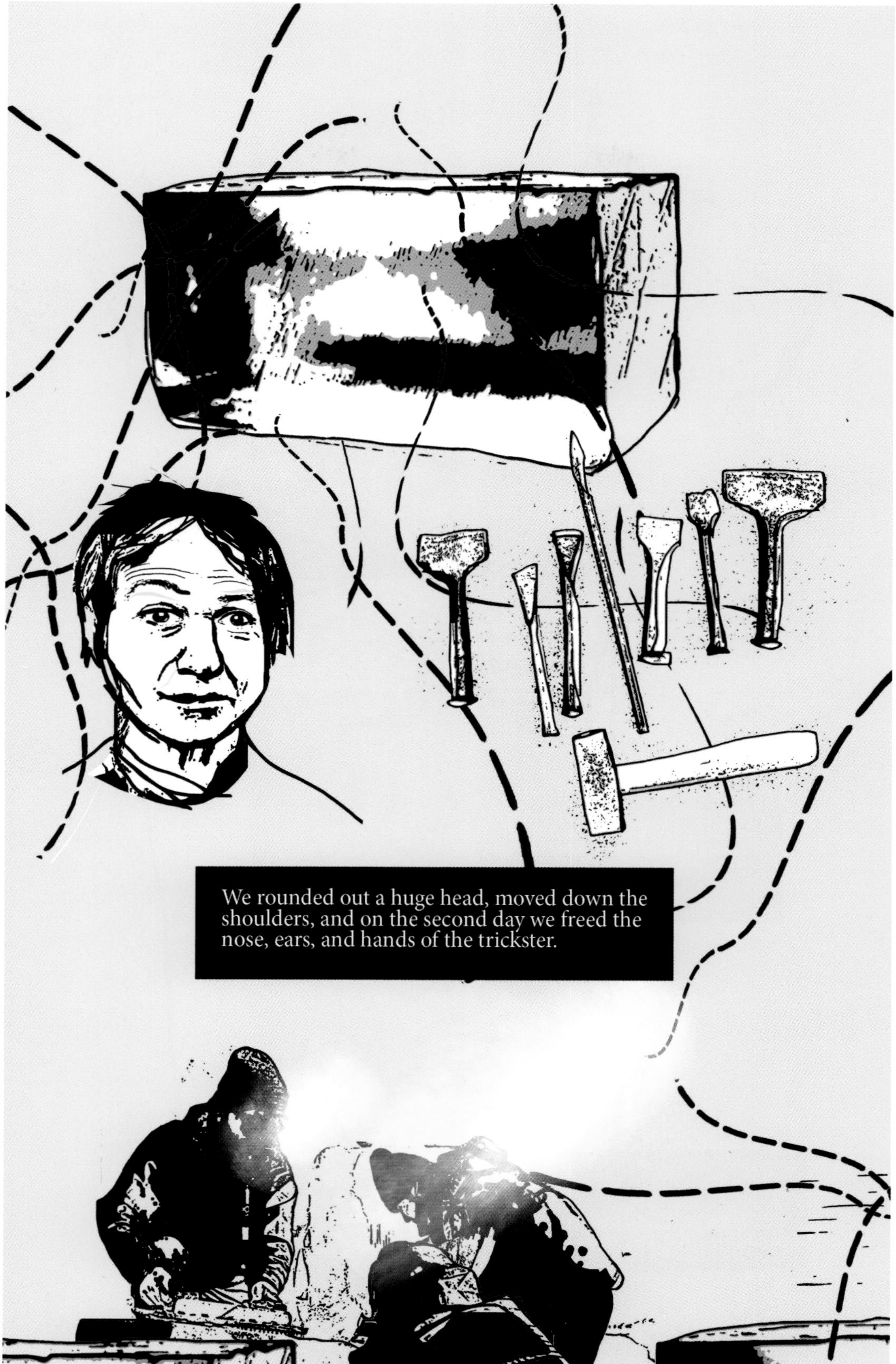
We rounded out a huge head, moved down the shoulders, and on the second day we freed the nose, ears, and hands of the trickster.

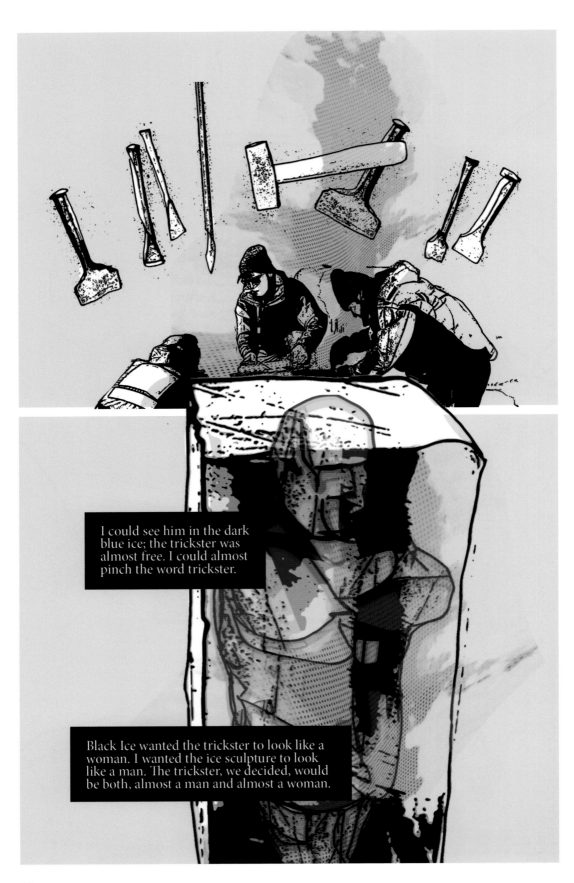

I could see him in the dark blue ice; the trickster was almost free. I could almost pinch the word trickster.

Black Ice wanted the trickster to look like a woman. I wanted the ice sculpture to look like a man. The trickster, we decided, would be both, almost a man and almost a woman.

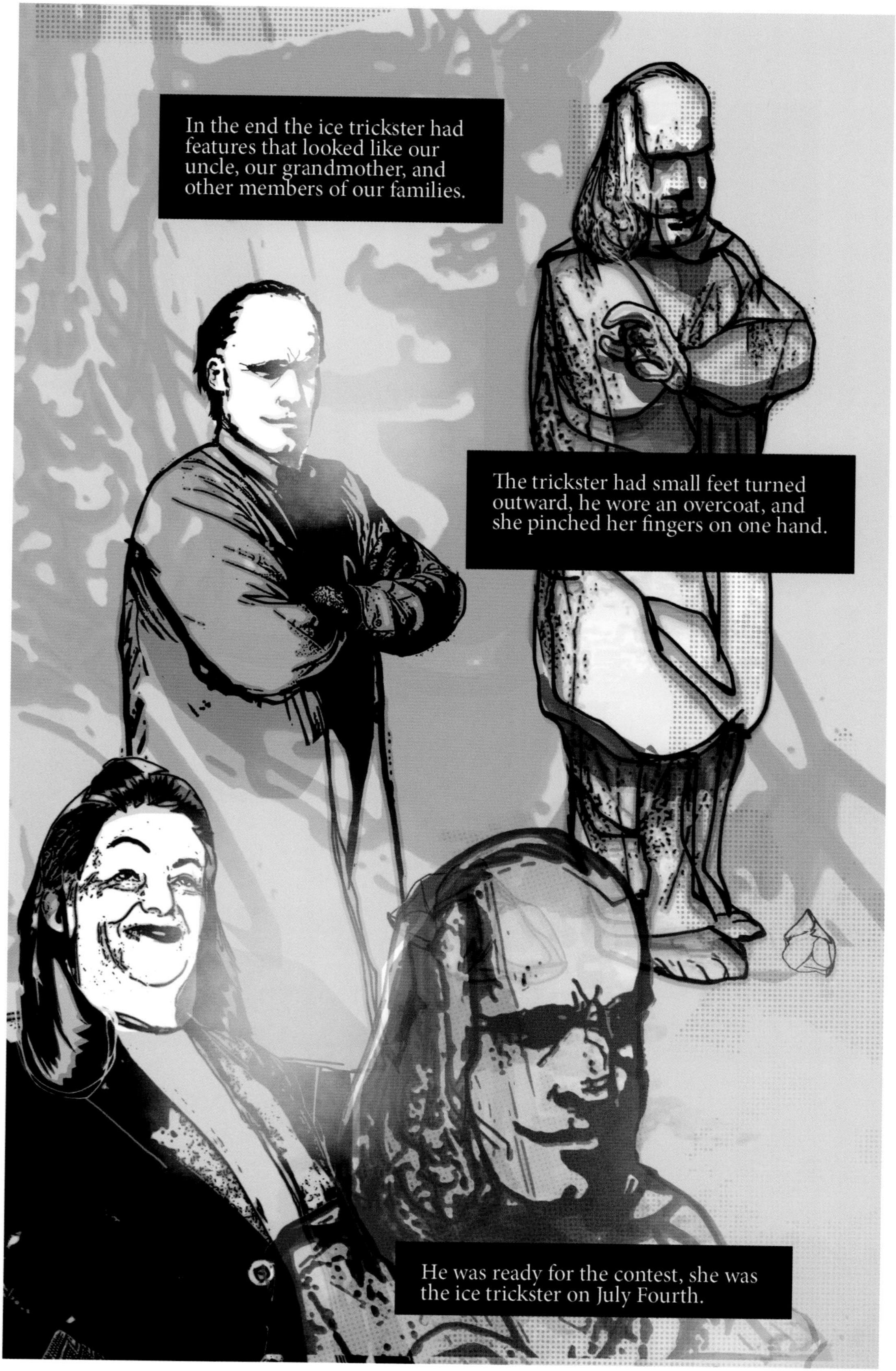
In the end the ice trickster had features that looked like our uncle, our grandmother, and other members of our families.
The trickster had small feet turned outward, he wore an overcoat, and she pinched her fingers on one hand.
He was ready for the contest, she was the ice trickster on July Fourth.

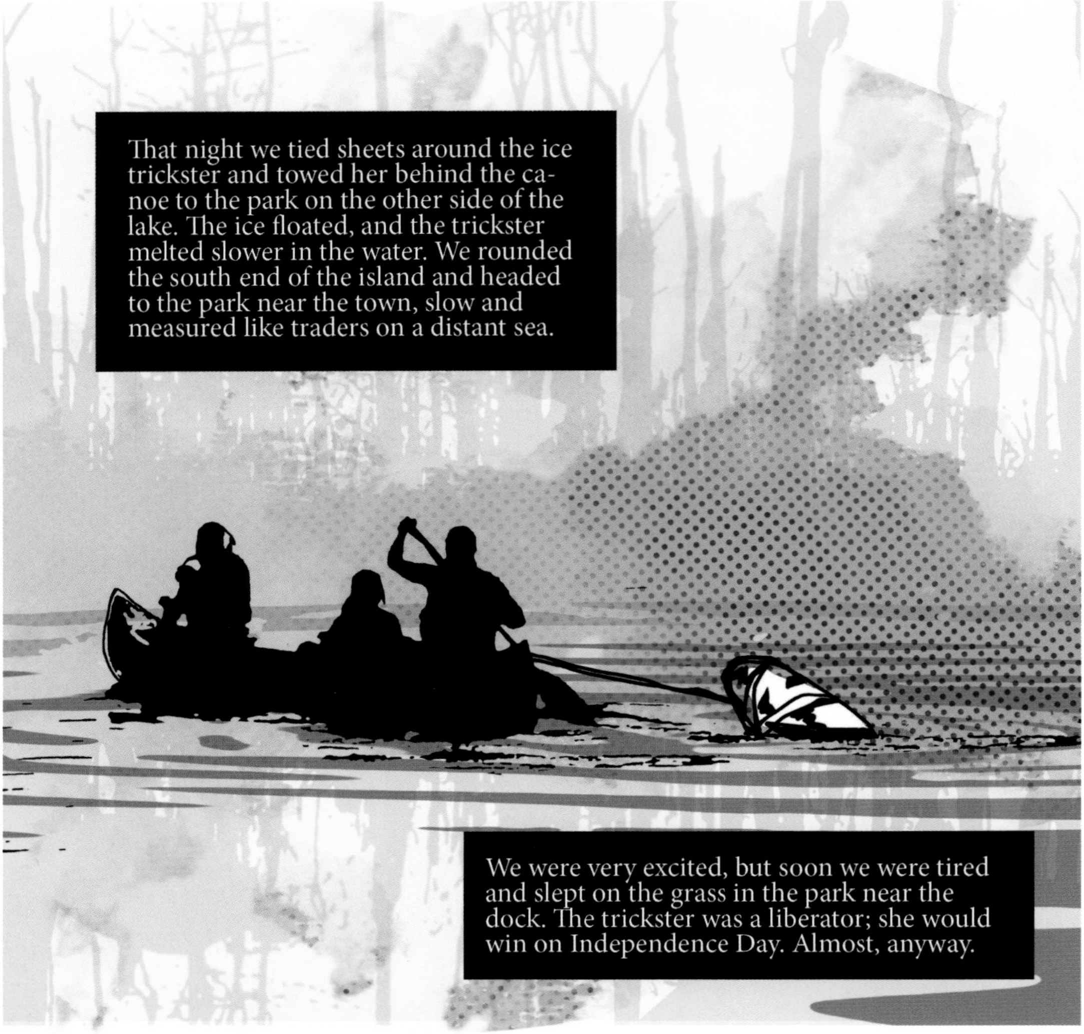
That night we tied sheets around the ice trickster and towed her behind the canoe to the park on the other side of the lake. The ice floated, and the trickster melted slower in the water. We rounded the south end of the island and headed to the park near the town, slow and measured like traders on a distant sea.
We were very excited, but soon we were tired and slept on the grass in the park near the dock. The trickster was a liberator; she would win on Independence Day. Almost, anyway.

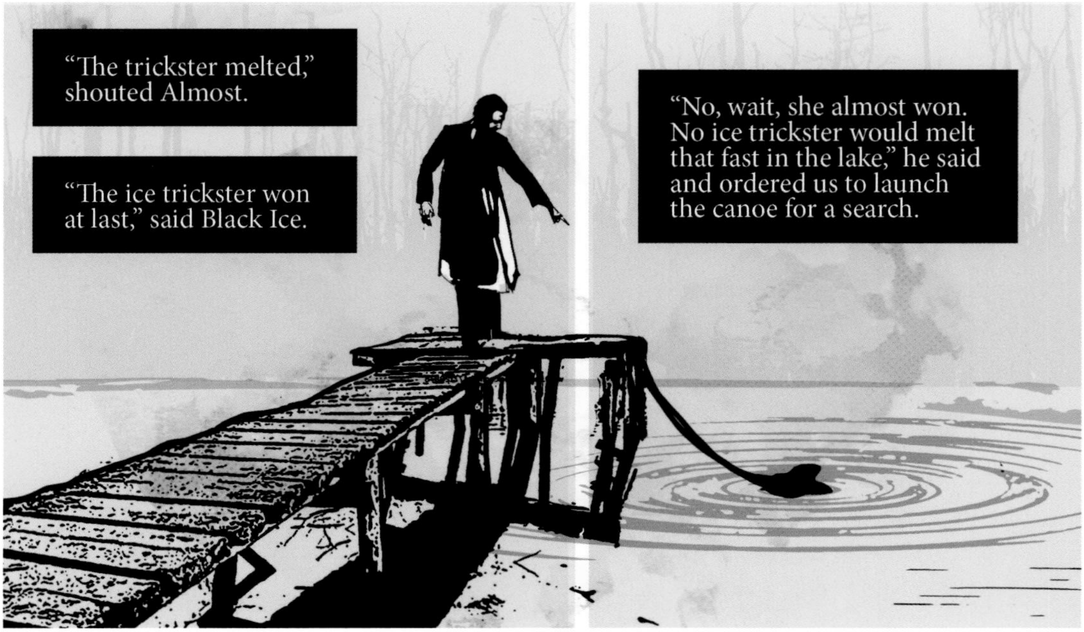
"The trickster melted," shouted Almost.
"The ice trickster won at last," said Black Ice.
"No, wait, she almost won. No ice trickster would melt that fast in the lake," he said and ordered us to launch the canoe for a search.

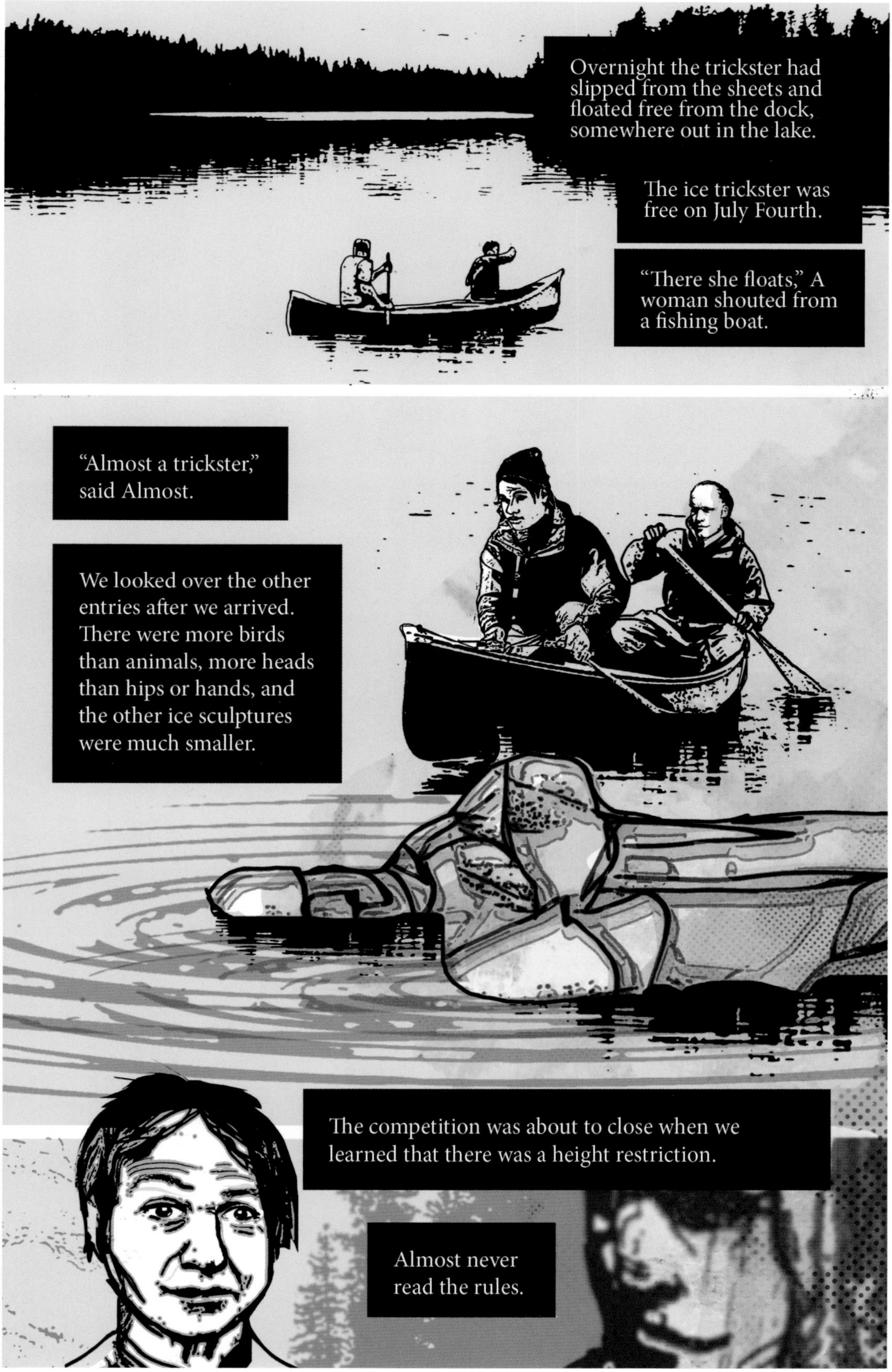
Overnight the trickster had slipped from the sheets and floated free from the dock, somewhere out in the lake.
The ice trickster was free on July Fourth.
"There she floats," A woman shouted from a fishing boat.
"Almost a trickster," said Almost.
We looked over the other entries after we arrived. There were more birds than animals, more heads than hips or hands, and the other ice sculptures were much smaller.
The competition was about to close when we learned that there was a height restriction.
Almost never read the rules.

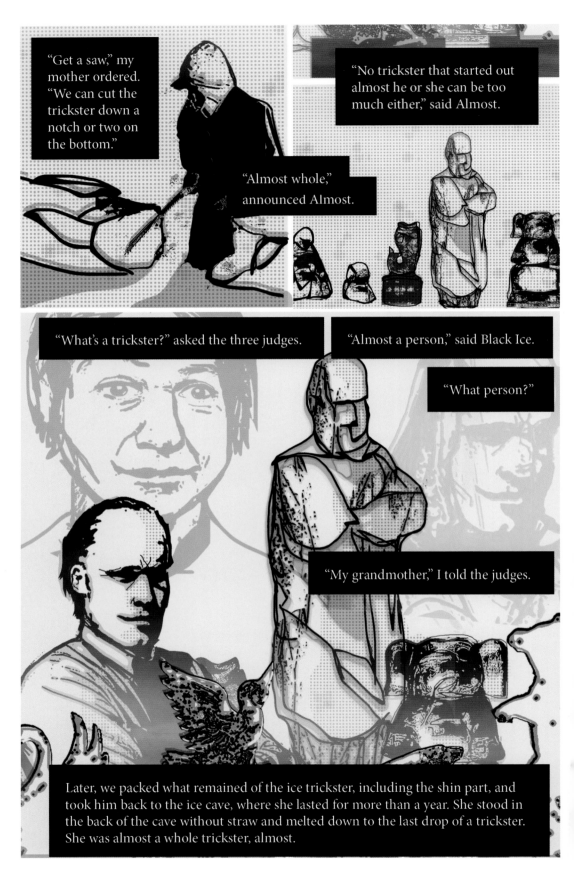

"Get a saw," my mother ordered. "We can cut the trickster down a notch or two on the bottom."

"No trickster that started out almost he or she can be too much either," said Almost.

"Almost whole," announced Almost.

"What's a trickster?" asked the three judges.

"Almost a person," said Black Ice.

"What person?"

"My grandmother," I told the judges.

Later, we packed what remained of the ice trickster, including the shin part, and took him back to the ice cave, where she lasted for more than a year. She stood in the back of the cave without straw and melted down to the last drop of a trickster. She was almost a whole trickster, almost.

An Athabasca Story

Warren Cariou

ILLUSTRATION & COLORS: Nicholas Burns

Warren Cariou was born in Meadow Lake, Saskatchewan, into a family of mixed Métis and European heritage. Though he has lived away from Meadow Lake for many years, his art and academic work maintains a focus on the cultural and environmental questions that have preoccupied the people of his homeland. His books, films, photography, and scholarly research explore themes of community, environment, orality, and belonging in the Canadian west, with particular focus on the relationships between Indigenous people and non-Native people. Cariou's books, including *The Exalted Company of Roadside Martyrs* and *Lake of the Prairies: A Story of Belonging*, have won and been nominated for numerous awards, including the Charles Taylor Prize for Literary Nonfiction and the Drainie-Taylor Prize for biography. He has also edited or coedited *W'daub Awae: Speaking True* and *Manitowapow: Aboriginal Stories from the Land of Water*. He holds a Canada Research Chair in Narrative, Community and Indigenous Cultures at the University of Manitoba, where he also teaches in the Department of English, Film and Theatre and directs the Centre for Creative Writing and Oral Culture.

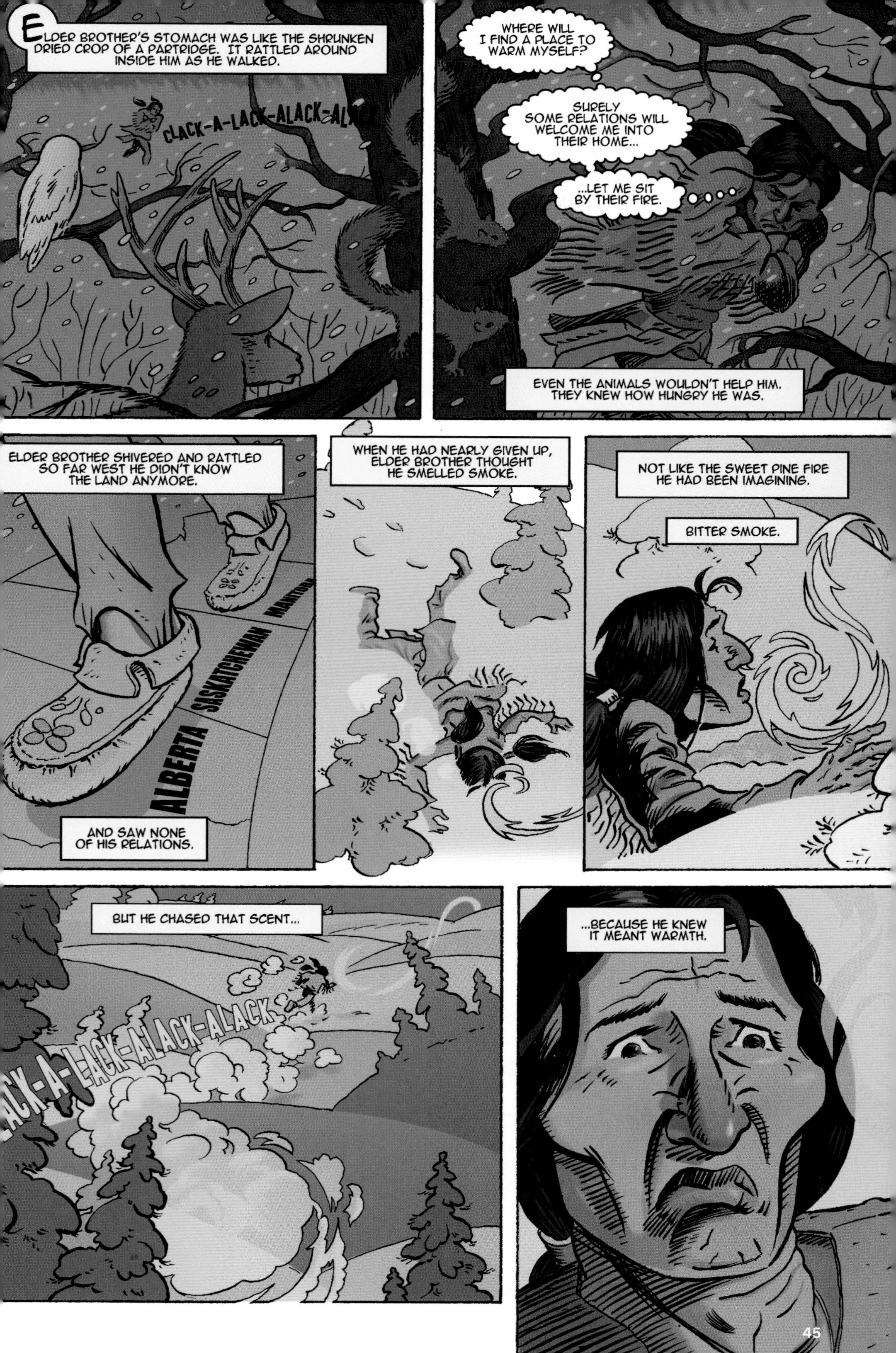
ELDER BROTHER'S STOMACH WAS LIKE THE SHRUNKEN DRIED CROP OF A PARTRIDGE. IT RATTLED AROUND INSIDE HIM AS HE WALKED.
CLACK-A-LACK-ALACK-ALACK
WHERE WILL I FIND A PLACE TO WARM MYSELF?
SURELY SOME RELATIONS WILL WELCOME ME INTO THEIR HOME...
...LET ME SIT BY THEIR FIRE.
EVEN THE ANIMALS WOULDN'T HELP HIM. THEY KNEW HOW HUNGRY HE WAS.
ELDER BROTHER SHIVERED AND RATTLED SO FAR WEST HE DIDN'T KNOW THE LAND ANYMORE.
MANITOBA
SASKATCHEWAN
ALBERTA
AND SAW NONE OF HIS RELATIONS.
WHEN HE HAD NEARLY GIVEN UP, ELDER BROTHER THOUGHT HE SMELLED SMOKE.
NOT LIKE THE SWEET PINE FIRE HE HAD BEEN IMAGINING.
BITTER SMOKE.
BUT HE CHASED THAT SCENT...
LACK-A-LACK-ALACK-ALACK
...BECAUSE HE KNEW IT MEANT WARMTH.

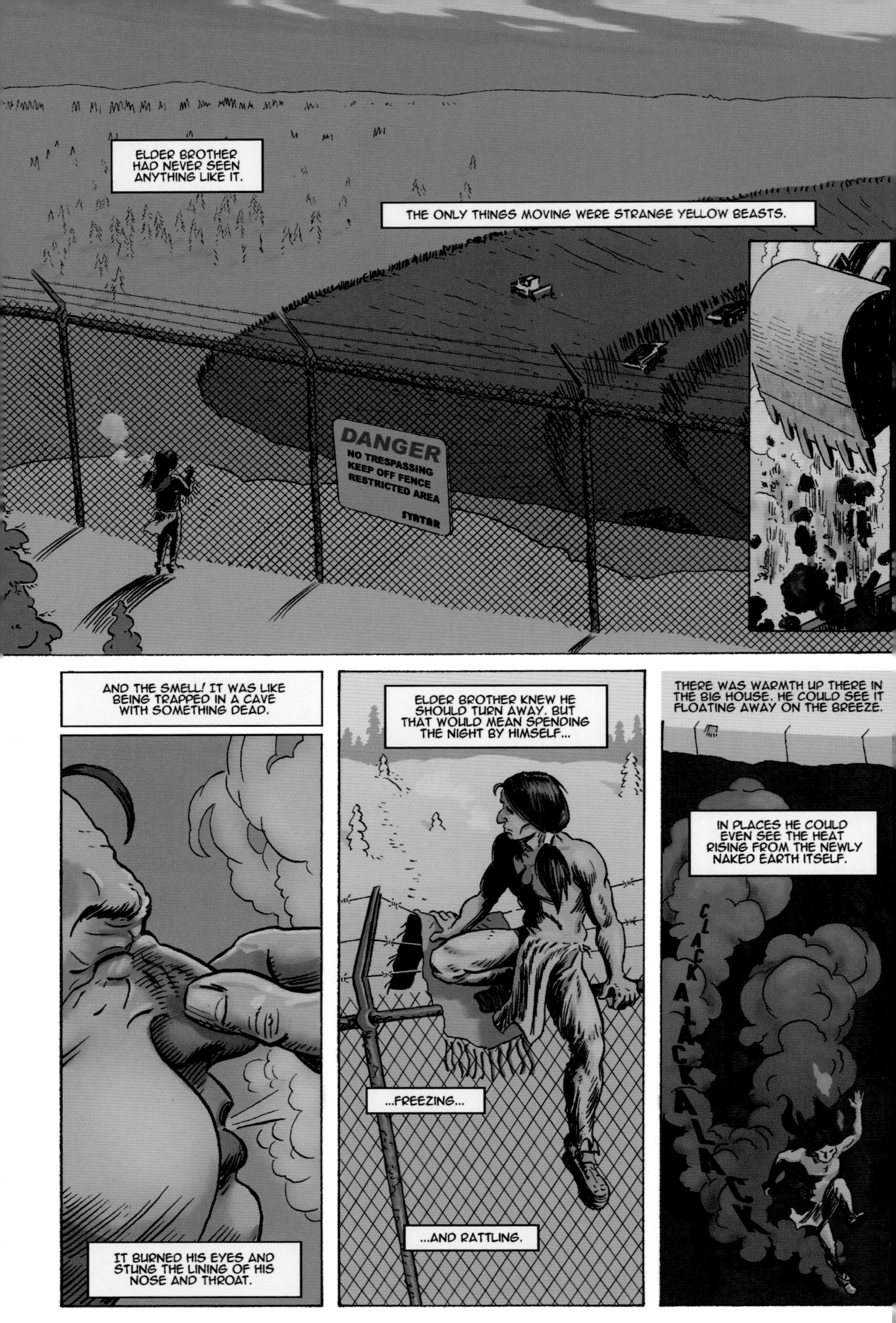
ELDER BROTHER HAD NEVER SEEN ANYTHING LIKE IT.
THE ONLY THINGS MOVING WERE STRANGE YELLOW BEASTS.
DANGER
NO TRESPASSING
KEEP OFF FENCE
RESTRICTED AREA
SYNTAR
AND THE SMELL! IT WAS LIKE BEING TRAPPED IN A CAVE WITH SOMETHING DEAD.
IT BURNED HIS EYES AND STUNG THE LINING OF HIS NOSE AND THROAT.
ELDER BROTHER KNEW HE SHOULD TURN AWAY. BUT THAT WOULD MEAN SPENDING THE NIGHT BY HIMSELF...
...FREEZING...
...AND RATTLING.
THERE WAS WARMTH UP THERE IN THE BIG HOUSE. HE COULD SEE IT FLOATING AWAY ON THE BREEZE.
IN PLACES HE COULD EVEN SEE THE HEAT RISING FROM THE NEWLY NAKED EARTH ITSELF.
CLACKALACK

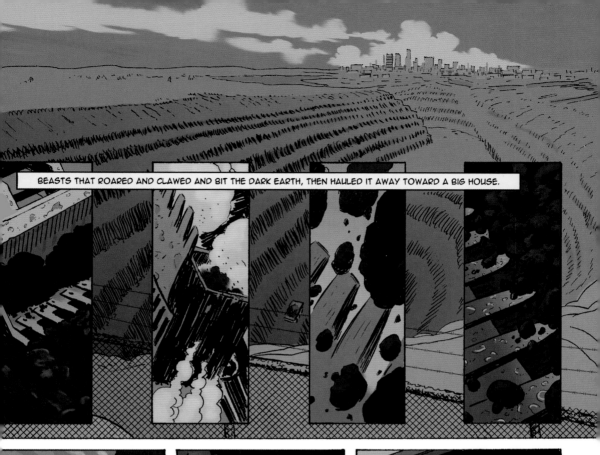

BEASTS THAT ROARED AND CLAWED AND BIT THE DARK EARTH, THEN HAULED IT AWAY TOWARD A BIG HOUSE.

WHAT STRANGE TRACKS.

AND THE BEASTS MAKE SMOKE TOO.

NOT BEASTS...

...HOUSES!

WARM, COMFORTABLE HOUSES THAT, BY SOME MAGIC, CAN *DIG* AND *HAUL* THE *EARTH!*

ROARRRRR!

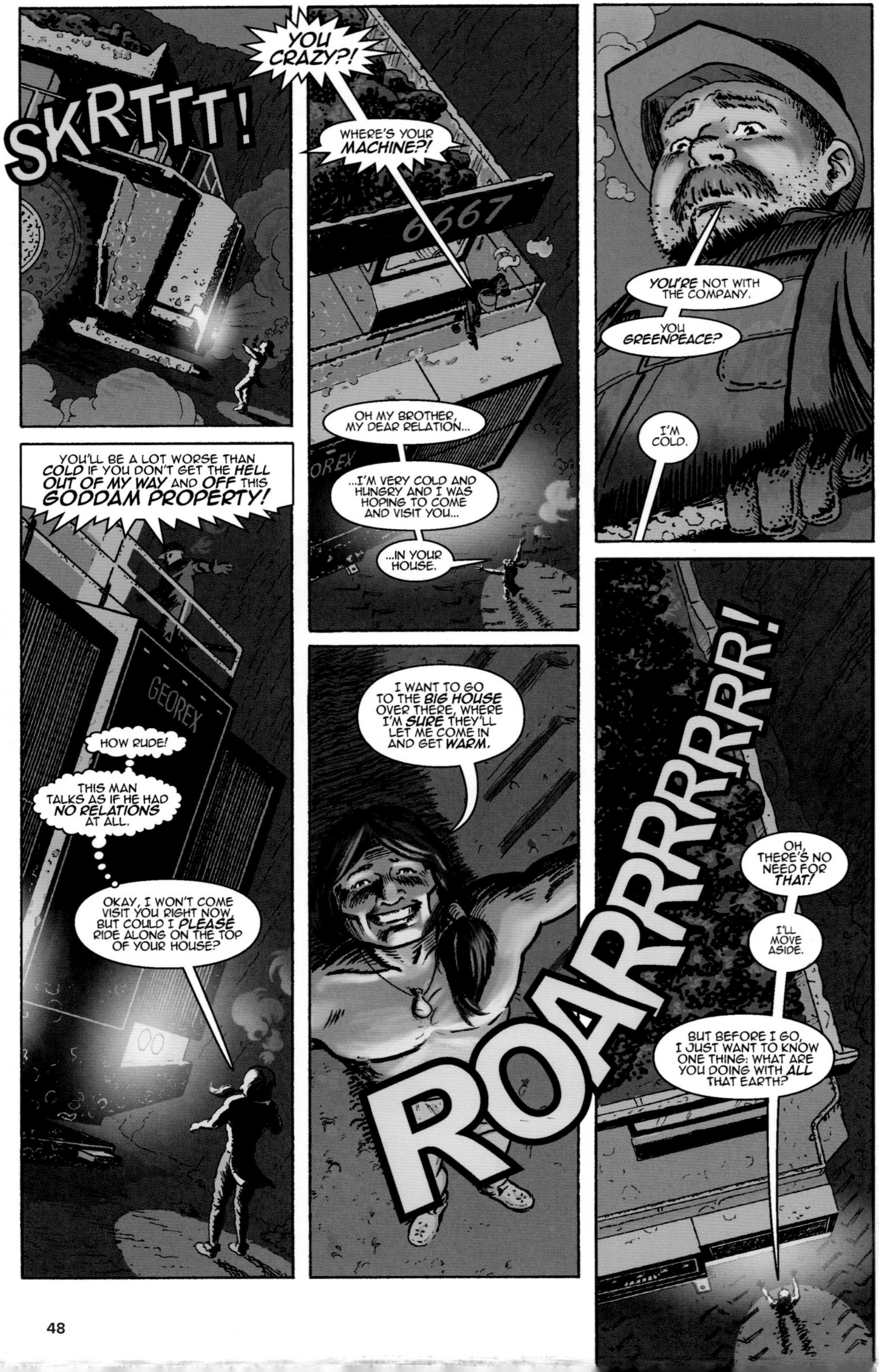
SKRTTT!
YOU CRAZY?!
WHERE'S YOUR MACHINE?!
6667
OH MY BROTHER, MY DEAR RELATION...
...I'M VERY COLD AND HUNGRY AND I WAS HOPING TO COME AND VISIT YOU...
...IN YOUR HOUSE.
YOU'RE NOT WITH THE COMPANY.
YOU GREENPEACE?
I'M COLD.
YOU'LL BE A LOT WORSE THAN COLD IF YOU DON'T GET THE HELL OUT OF MY WAY AND OFF THIS GODDAM PROPERTY!
GEOREX
HOW RUDE!
THIS MAN TALKS AS IF HE HAD NO RELATIONS AT ALL.
OKAY, I WON'T COME VISIT YOU RIGHT NOW, BUT COULD I PLEASE RIDE ALONG ON THE TOP OF YOUR HOUSE?
I WANT TO GO TO THE BIG HOUSE OVER THERE, WHERE I'M SURE THEY'LL LET ME COME IN AND GET WARM.
ROARRRRRRR!
OH, THERE'S NO NEED FOR THAT!
I'LL MOVE ASIDE.
BUT BEFORE I GO, I JUST WANT TO KNOW ONE THING: WHAT ARE YOU DOING WITH ALL THAT EARTH?

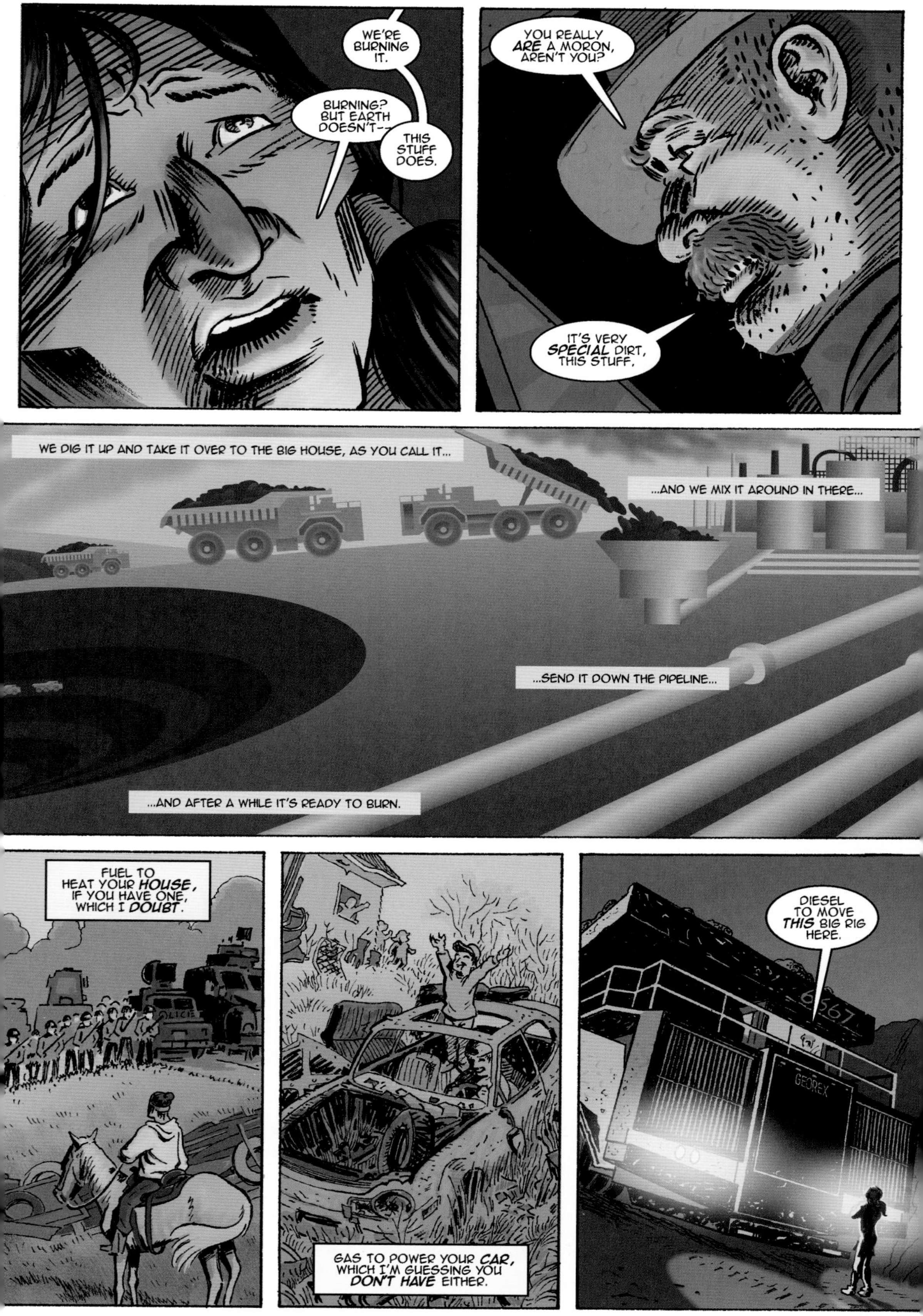
WE'RE BURNING IT.
BURNING? BUT EARTH DOESN'T--
THIS STUFF DOES.
YOU REALLY ARE A MORON, AREN'T YOU?
IT'S VERY SPECIAL DIRT, THIS STUFF.
WE DIG IT UP AND TAKE IT OVER TO THE BIG HOUSE, AS YOU CALL IT...
...AND WE MIX IT AROUND IN THERE...
...SEND IT DOWN THE PIPELINE...
...AND AFTER A WHILE IT'S READY TO BURN.
FUEL TO HEAT YOUR HOUSE, IF YOU HAVE ONE, WHICH I DOUBT.
GAS TO POWER YOUR CAR, WHICH I'M GUESSING YOU DON'T HAVE EITHER.
DIESEL TO MOVE THIS BIG RIG HERE.
GEOREX

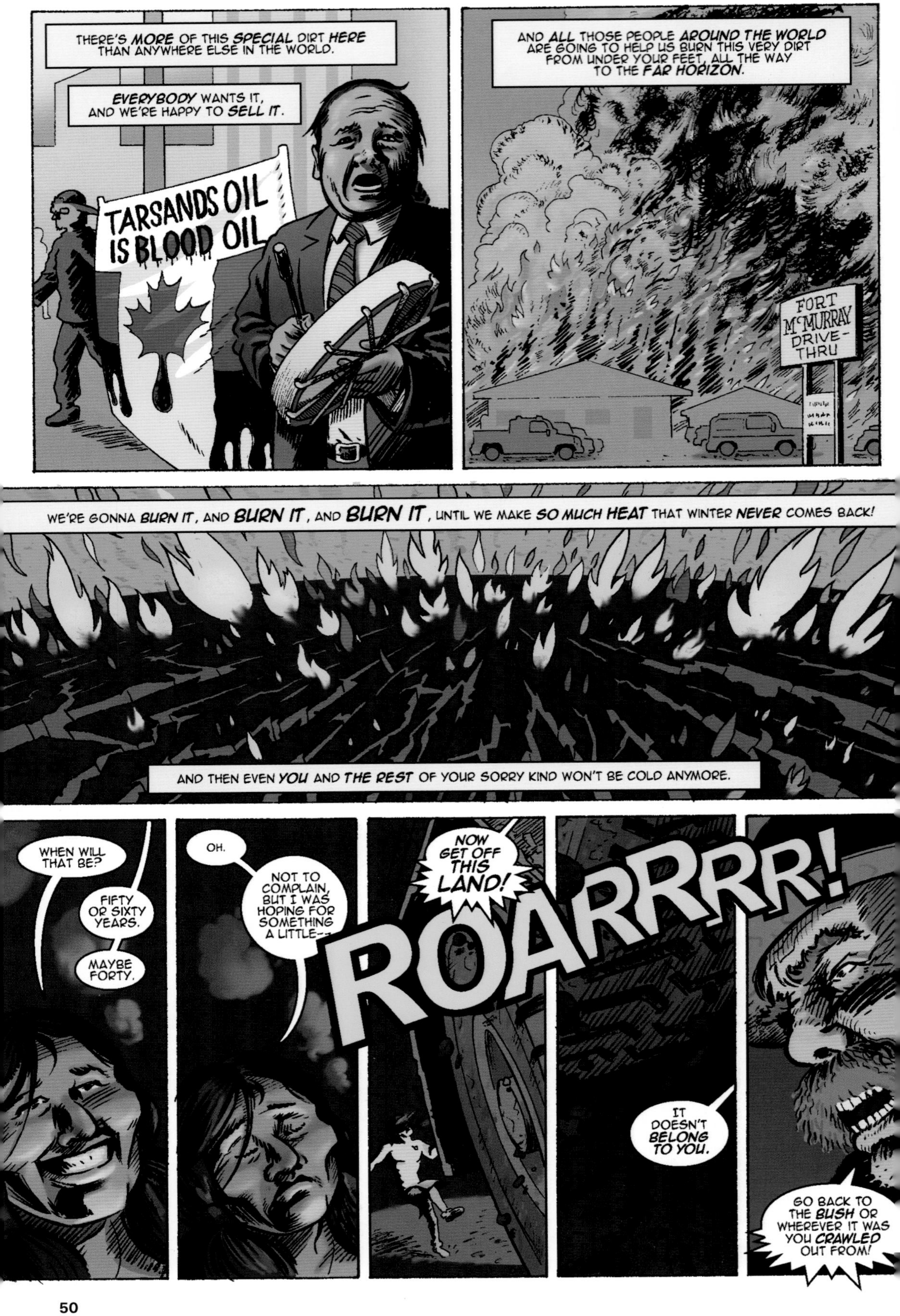
THERE'S MORE OF THIS SPECIAL DIRT HERE THAN ANYWHERE ELSE IN THE WORLD.
EVERYBODY WANTS IT, AND WE'RE HAPPY TO SELL IT.
TARSANDS OIL IS BLOOD OIL
AND ALL THOSE PEOPLE AROUND THE WORLD ARE GOING TO HELP US BURN THIS VERY DIRT FROM UNDER YOUR FEET, ALL THE WAY TO THE FAR HORIZON.
FORT McMURRAY DRIVE-THRU
WE'RE GONNA BURN IT, AND BURN IT, AND BURN IT, UNTIL WE MAKE SO MUCH HEAT THAT WINTER NEVER COMES BACK!
AND THEN EVEN YOU AND THE REST OF YOUR SORRY KIND WON'T BE COLD ANYMORE.
WHEN WILL THAT BE?
FIFTY OR SIXTY YEARS.
MAYBE FORTY.
OH.
NOT TO COMPLAIN, BUT I WAS HOPING FOR SOMETHING A LITTLE--
NOW GET OFF THIS LAND!
ROARRRRR!
IT DOESN'T BELONG TO YOU.
GO BACK TO THE BUSH OR WHEREVER IT WAS YOU CRAWLED OUT FROM!

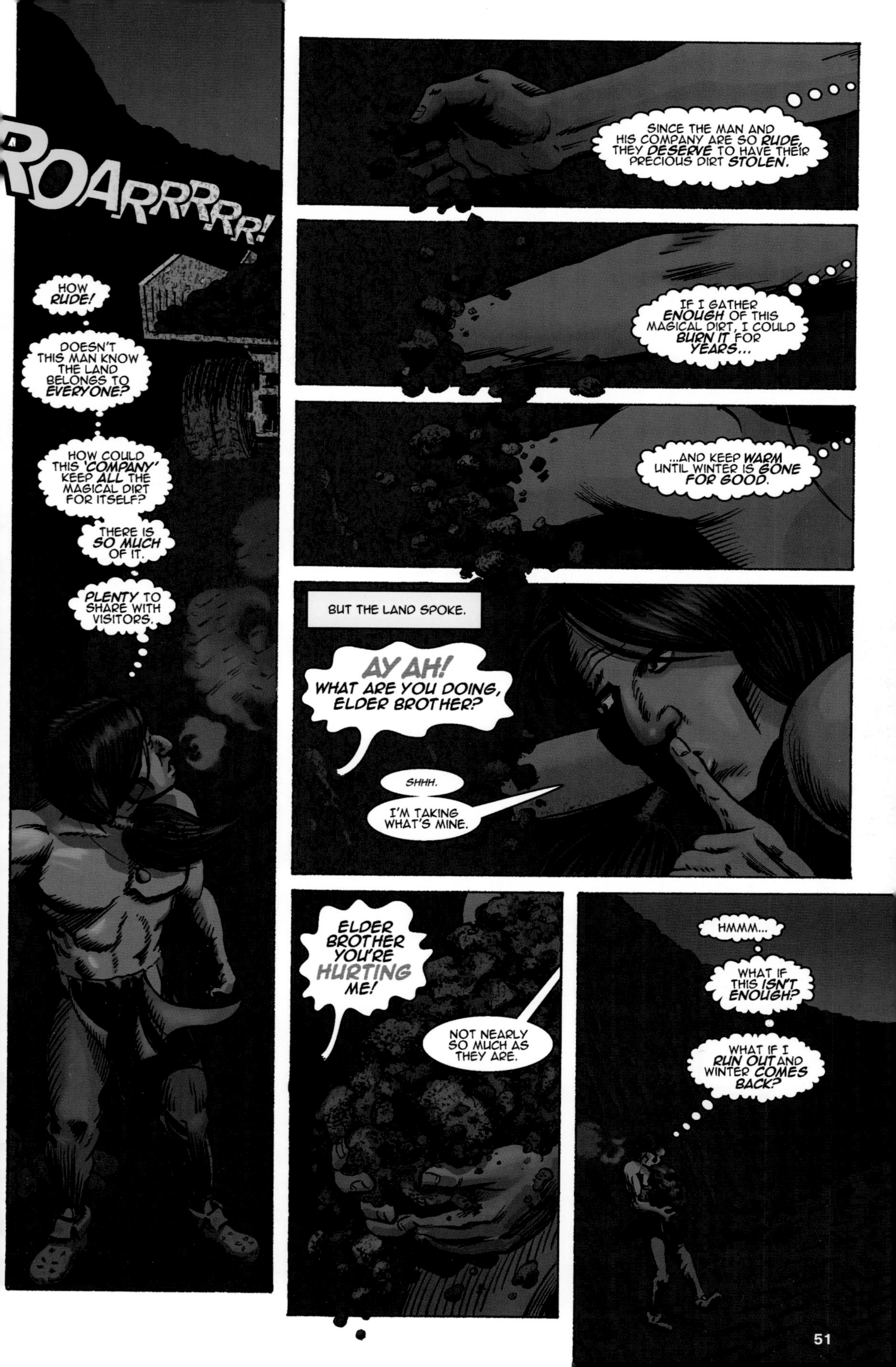
ROARRRRRR!
HOW RUDE!
DOESN'T THIS MAN KNOW THE LAND BELONGS TO EVERYONE?
HOW COULD THIS 'COMPANY' KEEP ALL THE MAGICAL DIRT FOR ITSELF?
THERE IS SO MUCH OF IT.
PLENTY TO SHARE WITH VISITORS.
SINCE THE MAN AND HIS COMPANY ARE SO RUDE, THEY DESERVE TO HAVE THEIR PRECIOUS DIRT STOLEN.
IF I GATHER ENOUGH OF THIS MAGICAL DIRT, I COULD BURN IT FOR YEARS...
...AND KEEP WARM UNTIL WINTER IS GONE FOR GOOD.
BUT THE LAND SPOKE.
AY AH! WHAT ARE YOU DOING, ELDER BROTHER?
SHHH.
I'M TAKING WHAT'S MINE.
ELDER BROTHER YOU'RE HURTING ME!
NOT NEARLY SO MUCH AS THEY ARE.
HMMM...
WHAT IF THIS ISN'T ENOUGH?
WHAT IF I RUN OUT AND WINTER COMES BACK?

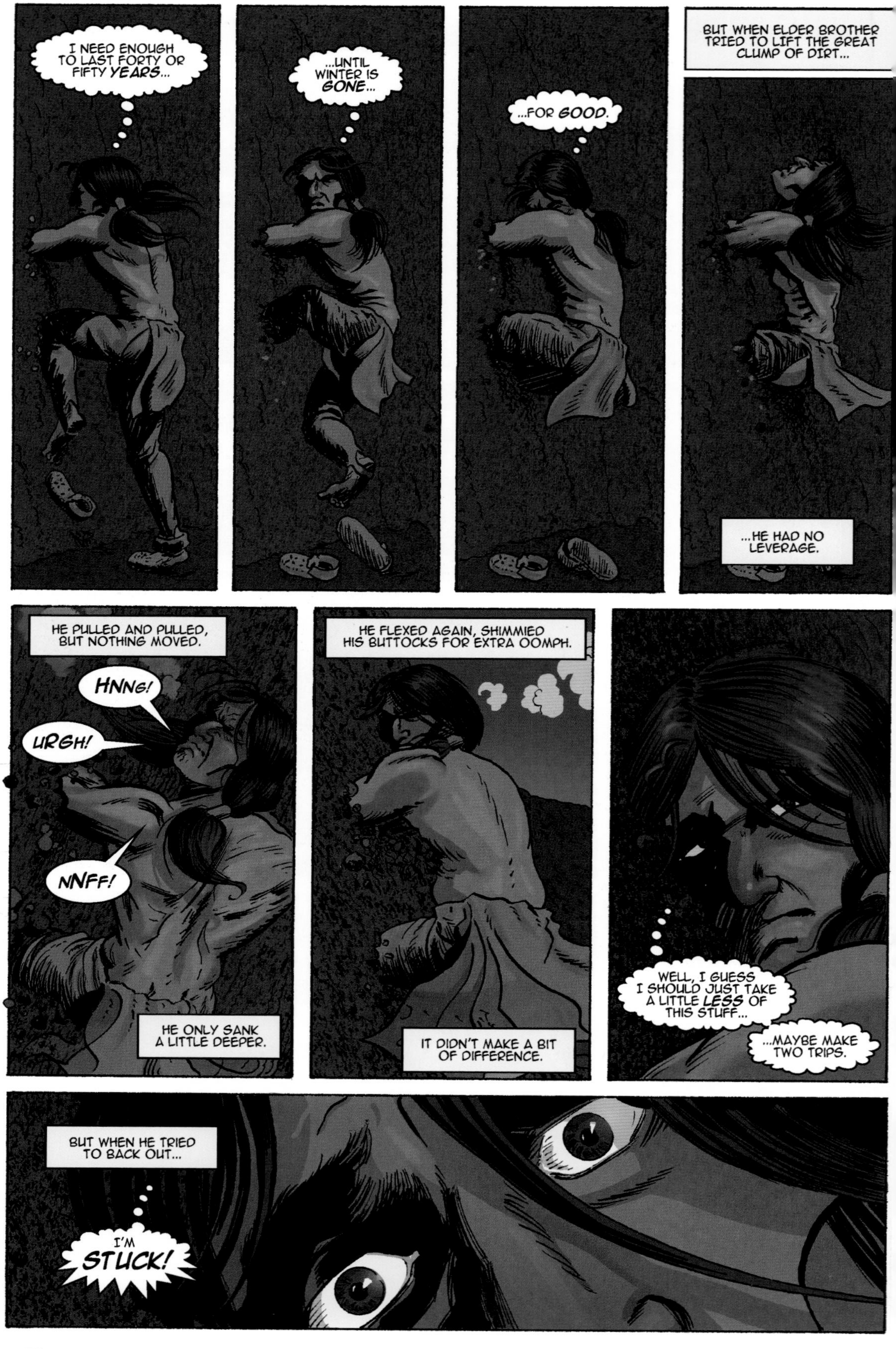
I NEED ENOUGH TO LAST FORTY OR FIFTY YEARS...
...UNTIL WINTER IS GONE...
...FOR GOOD.
BUT WHEN ELDER BROTHER TRIED TO LIFT THE GREAT CLUMP OF DIRT...
...HE HAD NO LEVERAGE.
HE PULLED AND PULLED, BUT NOTHING MOVED.
HNNG!
URGH!
NNFF!
HE ONLY SANK A LITTLE DEEPER.
HE FLEXED AGAIN, SHIMMIED HIS BUTTOCKS FOR EXTRA OOMPH.
IT DIDN'T MAKE A BIT OF DIFFERENCE.
WELL, I GUESS I SHOULD JUST TAKE A LITTLE LESS OF THIS STUFF...
...MAYBE MAKE TWO TRIPS.
BUT WHEN HE TRIED TO BACK OUT...
I'M STUCK!

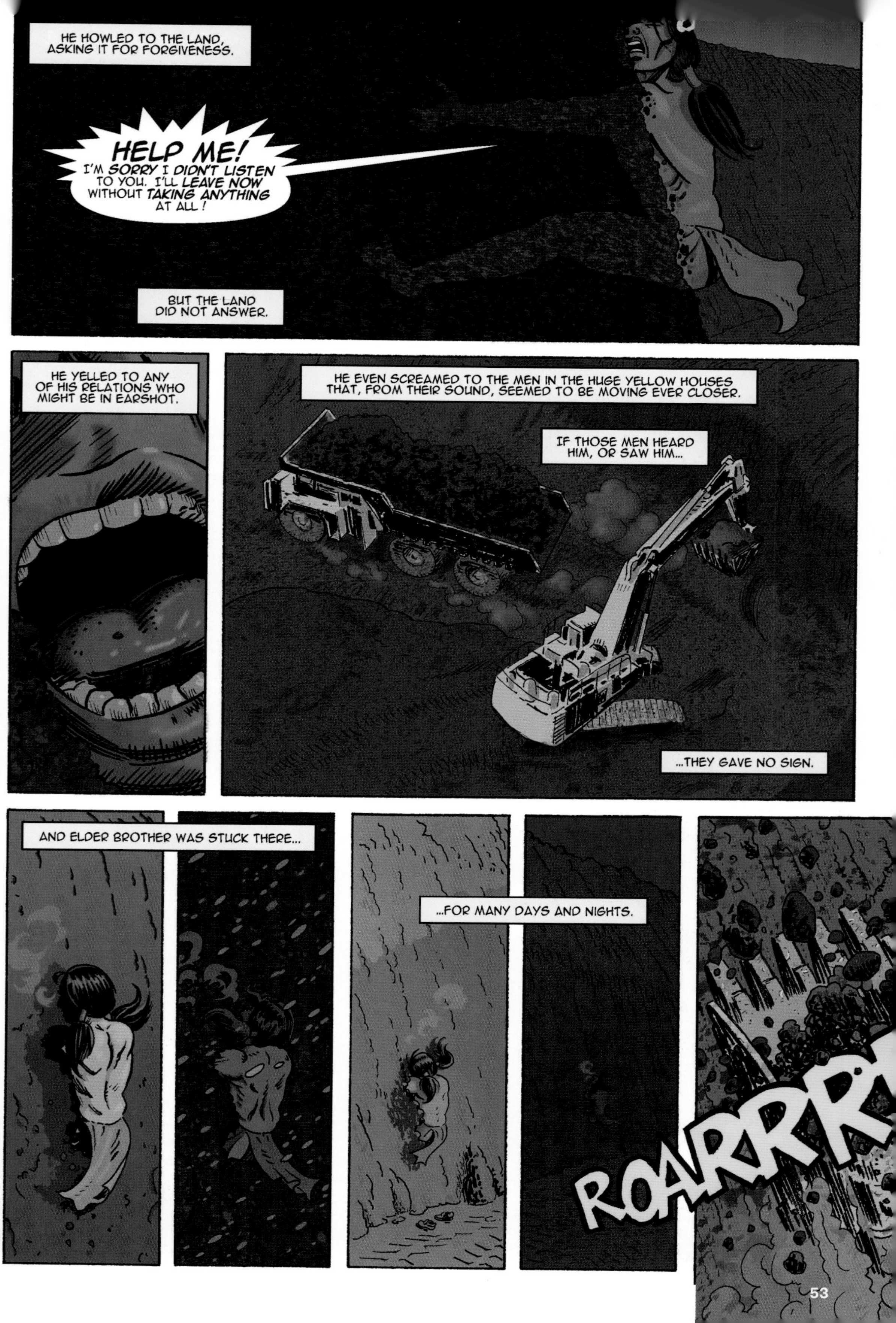
HE HOWLED TO THE LAND, ASKING IT FOR FORGIVENESS.
HELP ME! I'M SORRY I DIDN'T LISTEN TO YOU. I'LL LEAVE NOW WITHOUT TAKING ANYTHING AT ALL!
BUT THE LAND DID NOT ANSWER.
HE YELLED TO ANY OF HIS RELATIONS WHO MIGHT BE IN EARSHOT.
HE EVEN SCREAMED TO THE MEN IN THE HUGE YELLOW HOUSES THAT, FROM THEIR SOUND, SEEMED TO BE MOVING EVER CLOSER.
IF THOSE MEN HEARD HIM, OR SAW HIM...
...THEY GAVE NO SIGN.
AND ELDER BROTHER WAS STUCK THERE...
...FOR MANY DAYS AND NIGHTS.
ROARRR

HE FELT HIMSELF LIFTED, ALONG WITH HIS ARMLOAD OF DIRT AND A GREAT DEAL MORE.

HE FELT HIMSELF FALLING WITH THE THUNDEROUS SOUND OF EVERYTHING ELSE FALLING AROUND HIM.

AND HE CRIED OUT...

... BUT HE KNEW IT WAS HOPELESS. NO ONE WOULD HEAR HIM.

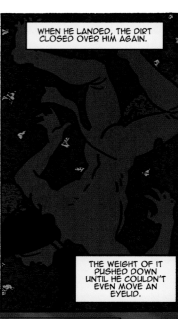

WHEN HE LANDED, THE DIRT CLOSED OVER HIM AGAIN.

THE WEIGHT OF IT PUSHED DOWN UNTIL HE COULDN'T EVEN MOVE AN EYELID.

HE WAS HAULED SLOWLY ACROSS THE WASTELAND, ENCASED THERE IN THE TAR SAND AS IF HE WERE A FOSSIL.

AND INSIDE THE REFINERY HE WAS MADE VERY WARM INDEED.

OF COURSE ELDER BROTHER CAN'T DIE, LUCKILY FOR HIM...

...OR PERHAPS NOT SO LUCKILY...

...AFTER EVERYTHING HE'S BEEN THROUGH.

IT'S TRUE THAT PEOPLE DON'T SEE HIM MUCH ANYMORE...

... BUT SOMETIMES, WHEN YOU PRESS HARD ON THE ACCELERATOR, YOU MIGHT HEAR A KNOCKING, RATTLING SOUND.

THAT'S ELDER BROTHER, TRYING TO GET YOUR ATTENTION...

...BEGGING YOU TO LET HIM OUT.

CLACK-A-LACK-ALACK-ALACK

THE END

Trickster Reflections

Niigaanwewidam James Sinclair

ILLUSTRATION & COLORS: GMB Chomichuk

Niigaanwewidam James Sinclair is Anishinaabe (St. Peter's/Little Peguis) and an Associate Professor at the University of Manitoba in the Department of Native Studies. He is an award-winning writer, editor, and activist who was named one of *Monocle Magazine*'s Canada's Top 20 Most Influential People and one of the CBC Manitoba's Top Forty Under Forty. His cowritten graphic novel *The Loxleys and Confederation* won the best illustrated and young adult books award at the 2016 Alberta Book Awards. He is a regular commentator on Indigenous issues on CTV, CBC, and APTN, and his written work can be found in the pages of newspapers like *The Guardian* and online with *CBC Books: Canada Writes*.

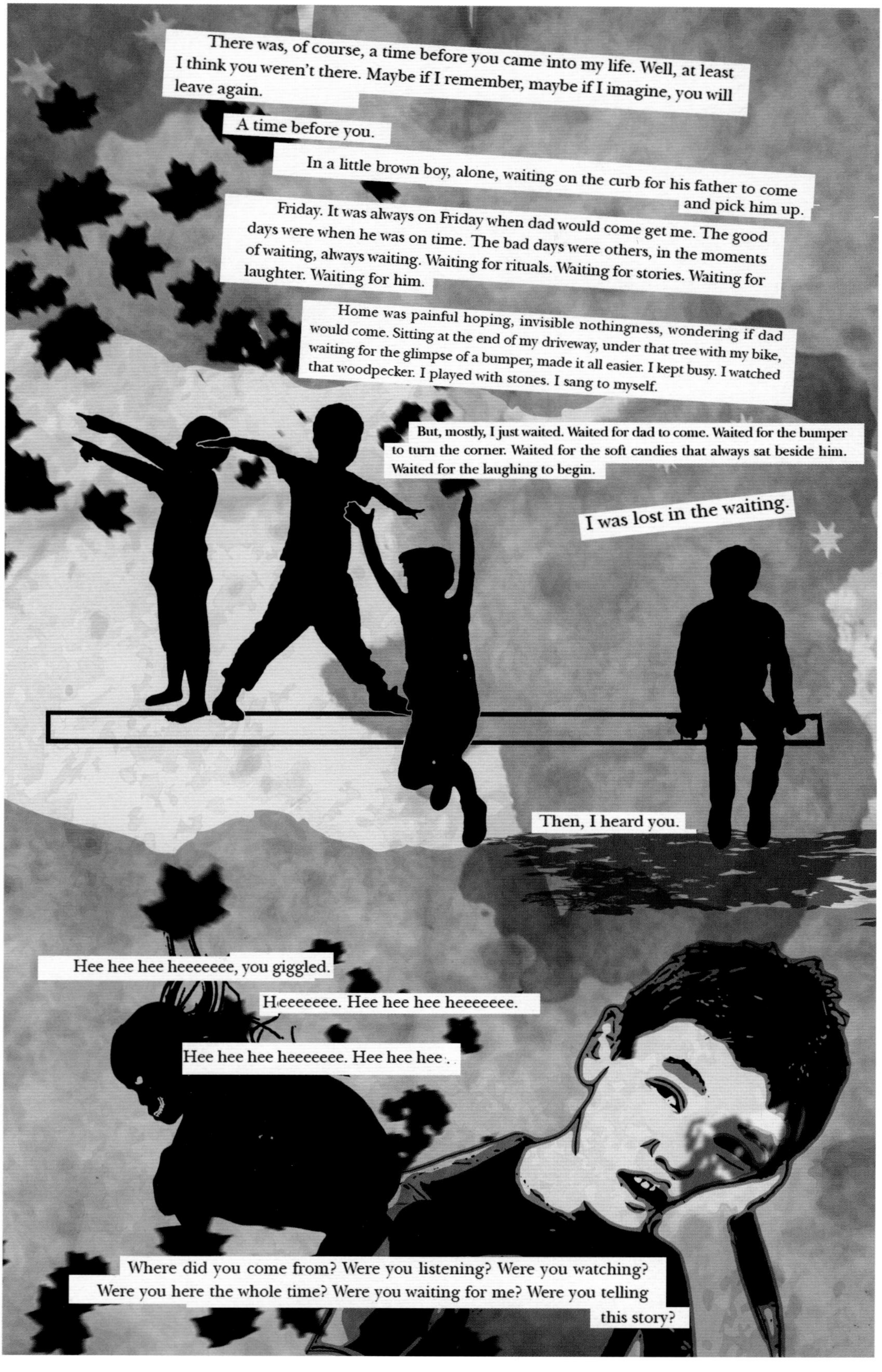
There was, of course, a time before you came into my life. Well, at least I think you weren't there. Maybe if I remember, maybe if I imagine, you will leave again.
A time before you.
In a little brown boy, alone, waiting on the curb for his father to come and pick him up.
Friday. It was always on Friday when dad would come get me. The good days were when he was on time. The bad days were others, in the moments of waiting, always waiting. Waiting for rituals. Waiting for stories. Waiting for laughter. Waiting for him.
Home was painful hoping, invisible nothingness, wondering if dad would come. Sitting at the end of my driveway, under that tree with my bike, waiting for the glimpse of a bumper, made it all easier. I kept busy. I watched that woodpecker. I played with stones. I sang to myself.
But, mostly, I just waited. Waited for dad to come. Waited for the bumper to turn the corner. Waited for the soft candies that always sat beside him. Waited for the laughing to begin.
I was lost in the waiting.
Then, I heard you.
Hee hee hee heeeeeee, you giggled.
Heeeeeee. Hee hee hee heeeeeee.
Hee hee hee heeeeeee. Hee hee hee . . .
Where did you come from? Were you listening? Were you watching? Were you here the whole time? Were you waiting for me? Were you telling this story?

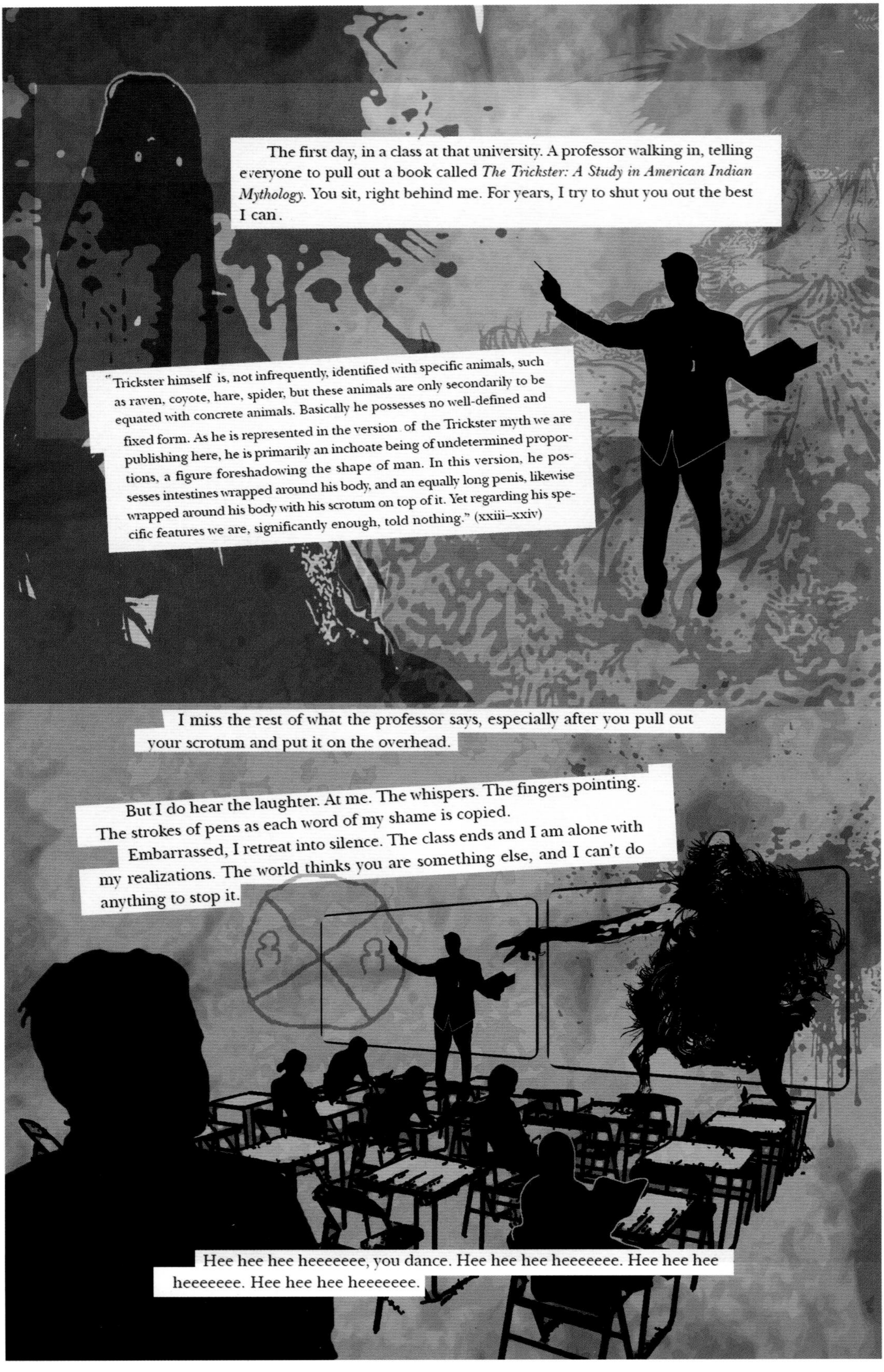
The first day, in a class at that university. A professor walking in, telling everyone to pull out a book called *The Trickster: A Study in American Indian Mythology*. You sit, right behind me. For years, I try to shut you out the best I can.
"Trickster himself is, not infrequently, identified with specific animals, such as raven, coyote, hare, spider, but these animals are only secondarily to be equated with concrete animals. Basically he possesses no well-defined and fixed form. As he is represented in the version of the Trickster myth we are publishing here, he is primarily an inchoate being of undetermined proportions, a figure foreshadowing the shape of man. In this version, he possesses intestines wrapped around his body, and an equally long penis, likewise wrapped around his body with his scrotum on top of it. Yet regarding his specific features we are, significantly enough, told nothing." (xxiii–xxiv)
I miss the rest of what the professor says, especially after you pull out your scrotum and put it on the overhead.
But I do hear the laughter. At me. The whispers. The fingers pointing. The strokes of pens as each word of my shame is copied.
Embarrassed, I retreat into silence. The class ends and I am alone with my realizations. The world thinks you are something else, and I can't do anything to stop it.
Hee hee hee heeeeeee, you dance. Hee hee hee heeeeeee. Hee hee hee heeeeeee. Hee hee hee heeeeeee.

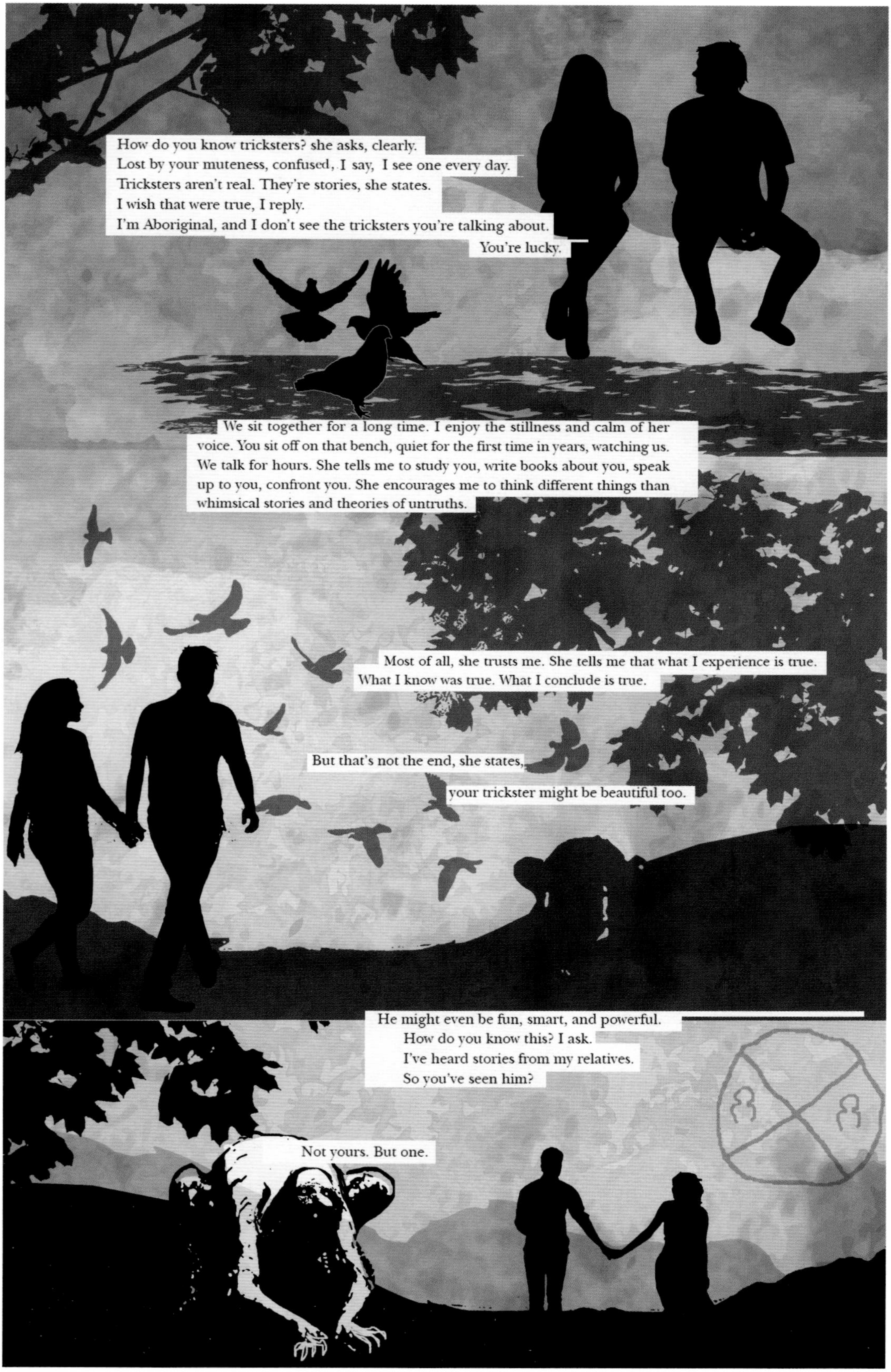
How do you know tricksters? she asks, clearly.
Lost by your muteness, confused, I say, I see one every day.
Tricksters aren't real. They're stories, she states.
I wish that were true, I reply.
I'm Aboriginal, and I don't see the tricksters you're talking about.
You're lucky.
We sit together for a long time. I enjoy the stillness and calm of her voice. You sit off on that bench, quiet for the first time in years, watching us. We talk for hours. She tells me to study you, write books about you, speak up to you, confront you. She encourages me to think different things than whimsical stories and theories of untruths.
Most of all, she trusts me. She tells me that what I experience is true. What I know was true. What I conclude is true.
But that's not the end, she states,
your trickster might be beautiful too.
He might even be fun, smart, and powerful.
How do you know this? I ask.
I've heard stories from my relatives.
So you've seen him?
Not yours. But one.

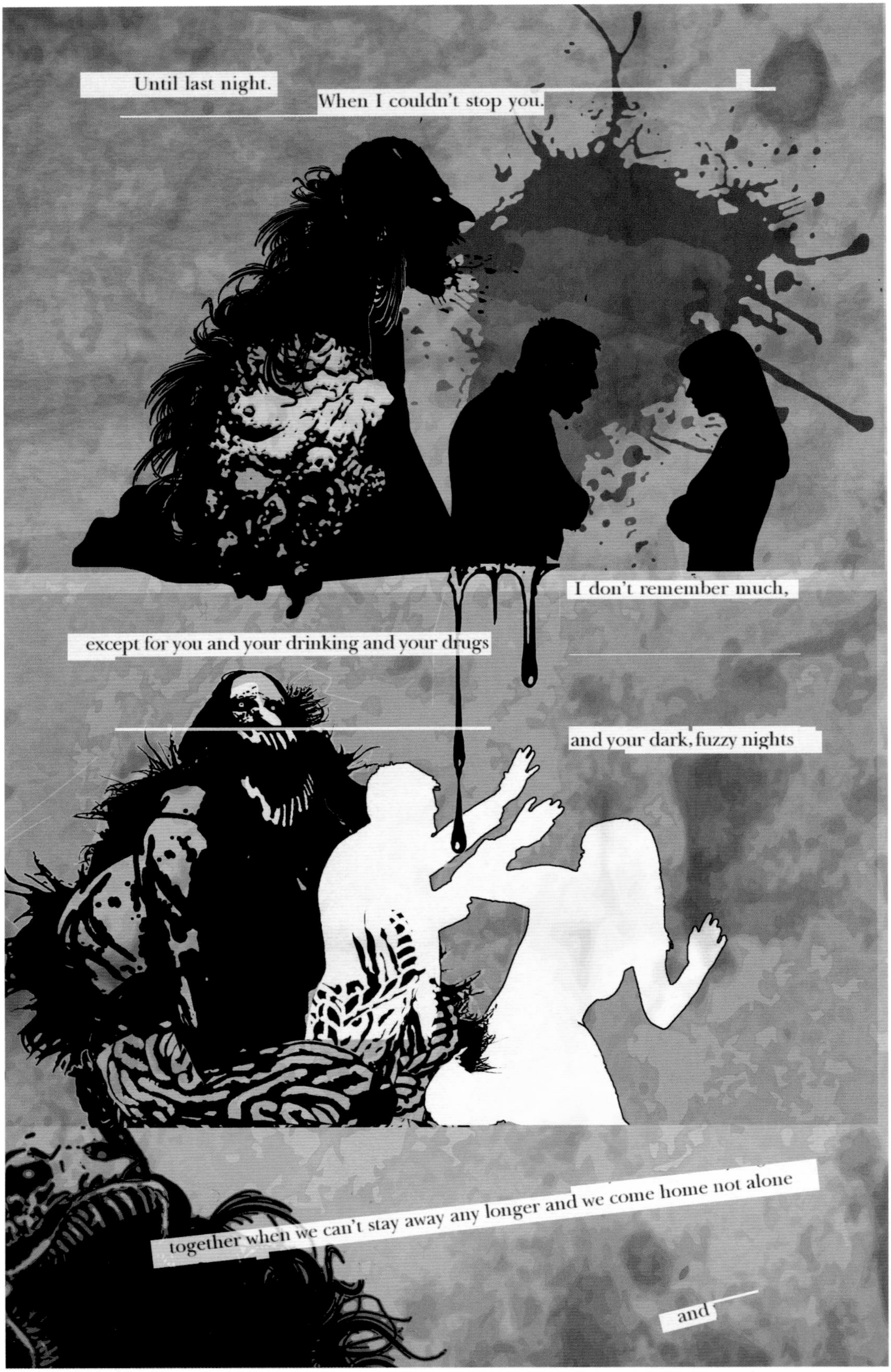
Until last night.
When I couldn't stop you.
I don't remember much,
except for you and your drinking and your drugs
and your dark, fuzzy nights
together when we can't stay away any longer and we come home not alone
and

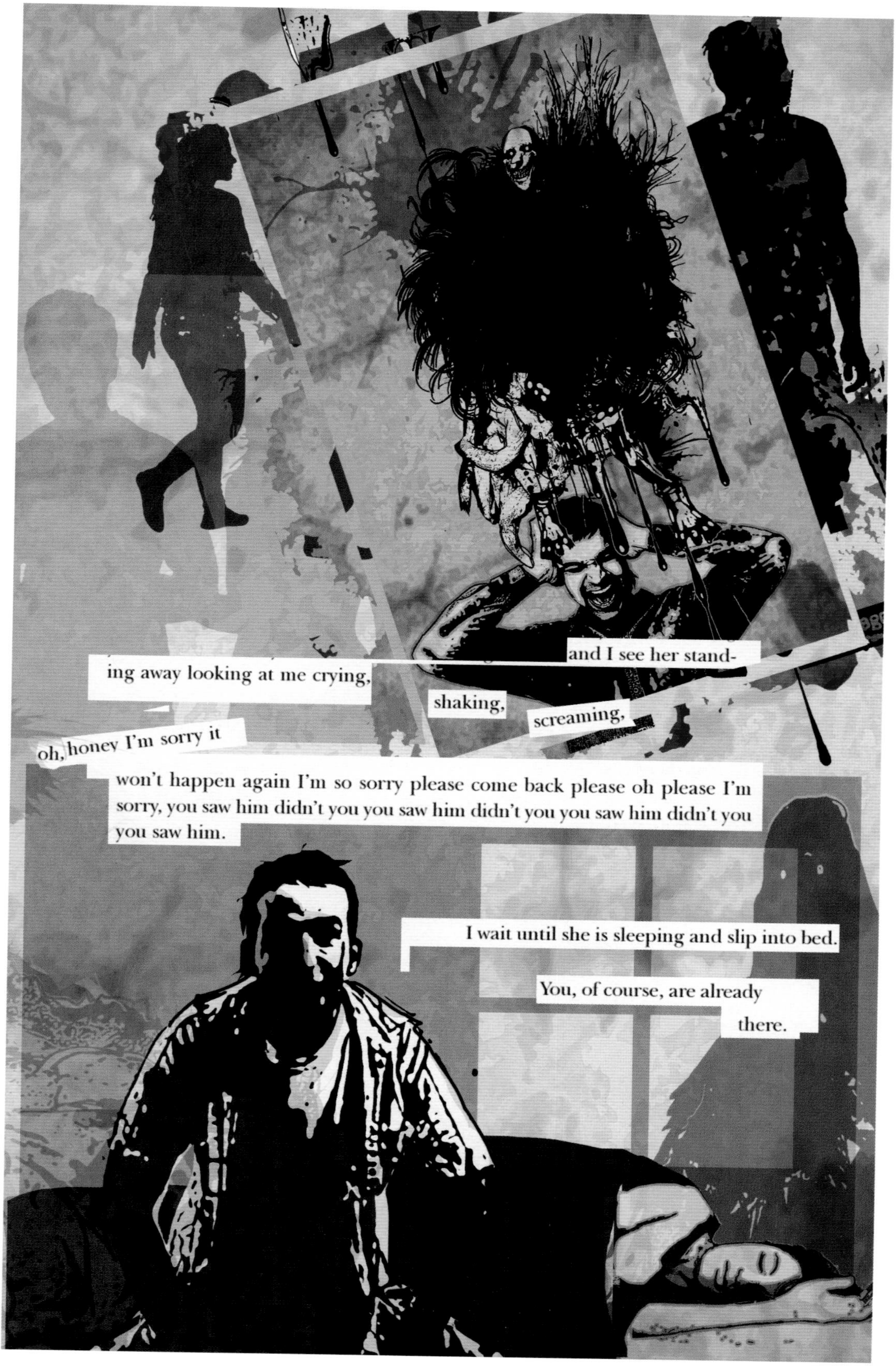
and I see her stand-
ing away looking at me crying,
shaking,
screaming,
oh, honey I'm sorry it
won't happen again I'm so sorry please come back please oh please I'm sorry, you saw him didn't you you saw him didn't you you saw him didn't you you saw him.
I wait until she is sleeping and slip into bed.
You, of course, are already
there.

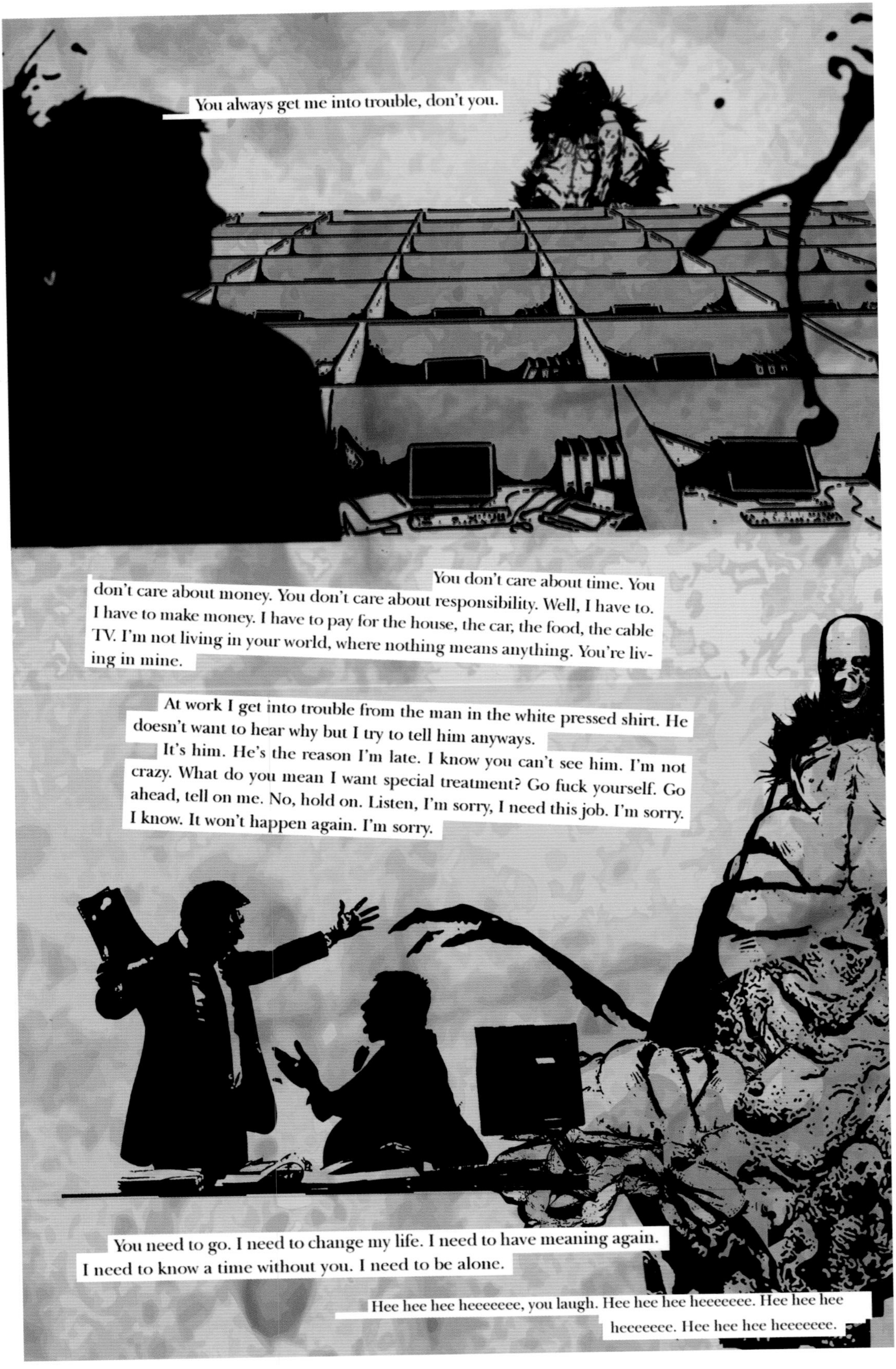
You always get me into trouble, don't you.
You don't care about time. You don't care about money. You don't care about responsibility. Well, I have to. I have to make money. I have to pay for the house, the car, the food, the cable TV. I'm not living in your world, where nothing means anything. You're living in mine.
At work I get into trouble from the man in the white pressed shirt. He doesn't want to hear why but I try to tell him anyways.
It's him. He's the reason I'm late. I know you can't see him. I'm not crazy. What do you mean I want special treatment? Go fuck yourself. Go ahead, tell on me. No, hold on. Listen, I'm sorry, I need this job. I'm sorry. I know. It won't happen again. I'm sorry.
You need to go. I need to change my life. I need to have meaning again. I need to know a time without you. I need to be alone.
Hee hee hee heeeeeee, you laugh. Hee hee hee heeeeeee. Hee hee hee heeeeeee. Hee hee hee heeeeeee.

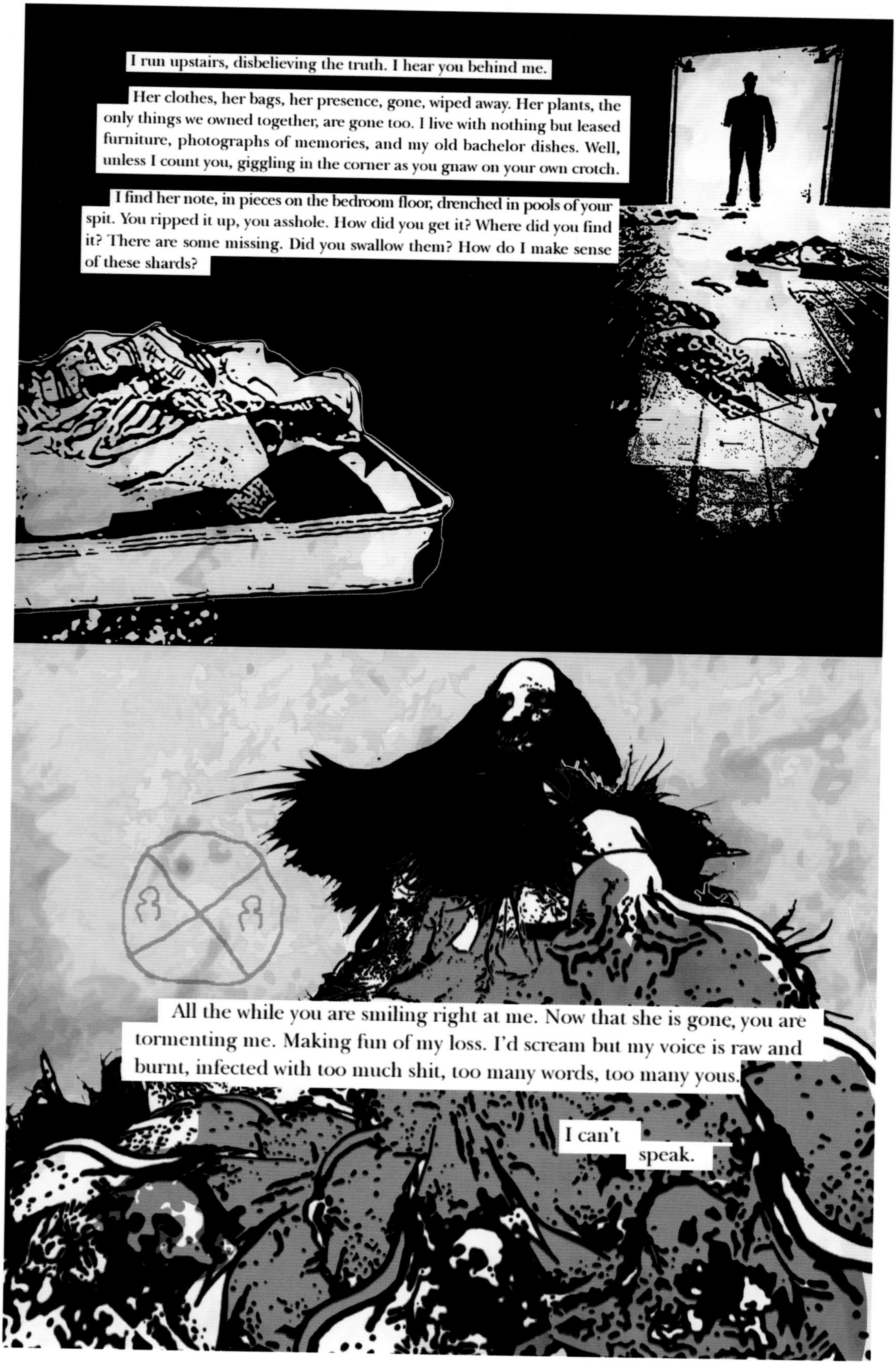
I run upstairs, disbelieving the truth. I hear you behind me.
Her clothes, her bags, her presence, gone, wiped away. Her plants, the only things we owned together, are gone too. I live with nothing but leased furniture, photographs of memories, and my old bachelor dishes. Well, unless I count you, giggling in the corner as you gnaw on your own crotch.
I find her note, in pieces on the bedroom floor, drenched in pools of your spit. You ripped it up, you asshole. How did you get it? Where did you find it? There are some missing. Did you swallow them? How do I make sense of these shards?
All the while you are smiling right at me. Now that she is gone, you are tormenting me. Making fun of my loss. I'd scream but my voice is raw and burnt, infected with too much shit, too many words, too many yous.
I can't
speak.

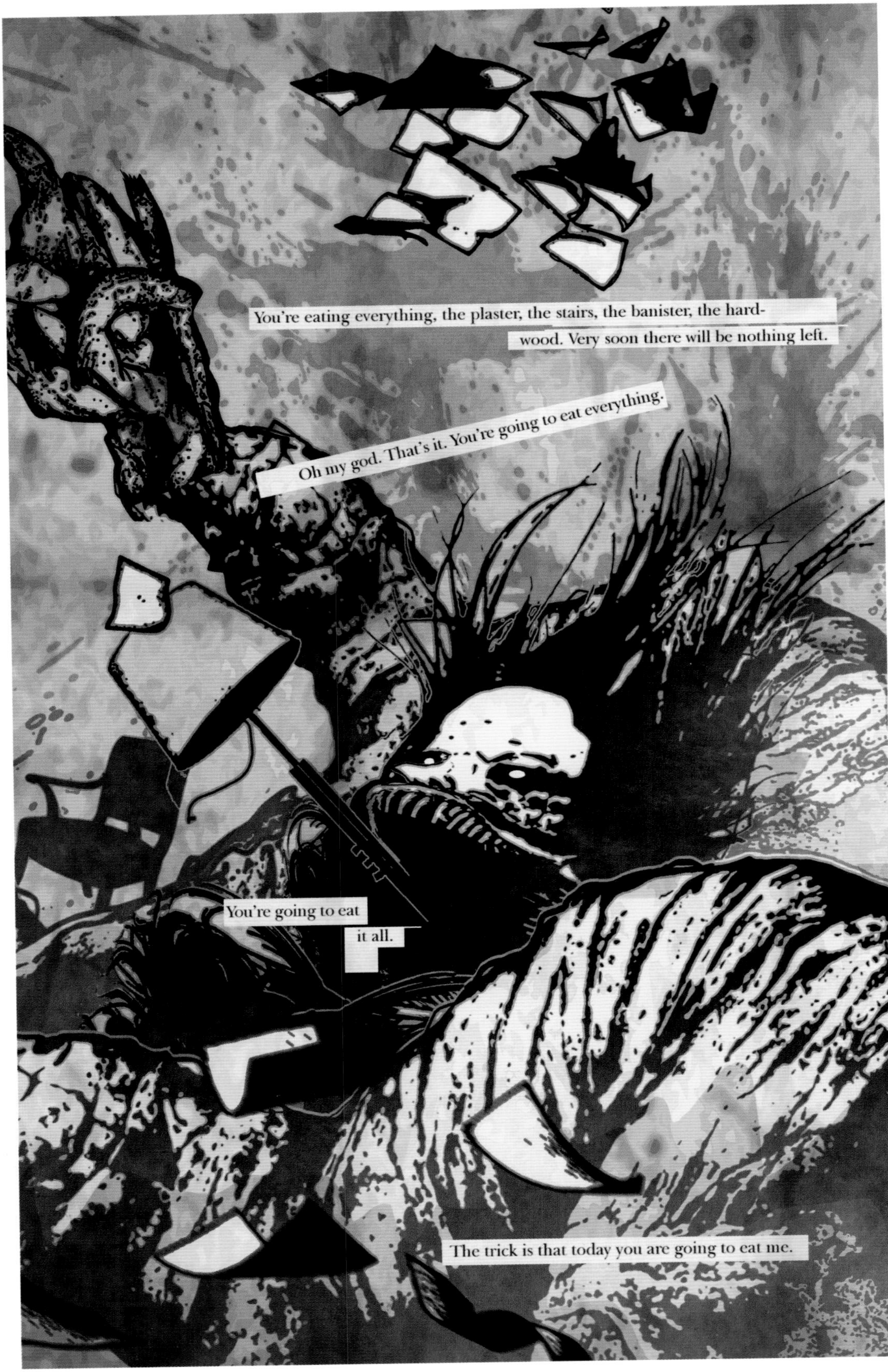
You're eating everything, the plaster, the stairs, the banister, the hard-
wood. Very soon there will be nothing left.
Oh my god. That's it. You're going to eat everything.
You're going to eat
it all.
The trick is that today you are going to eat me.

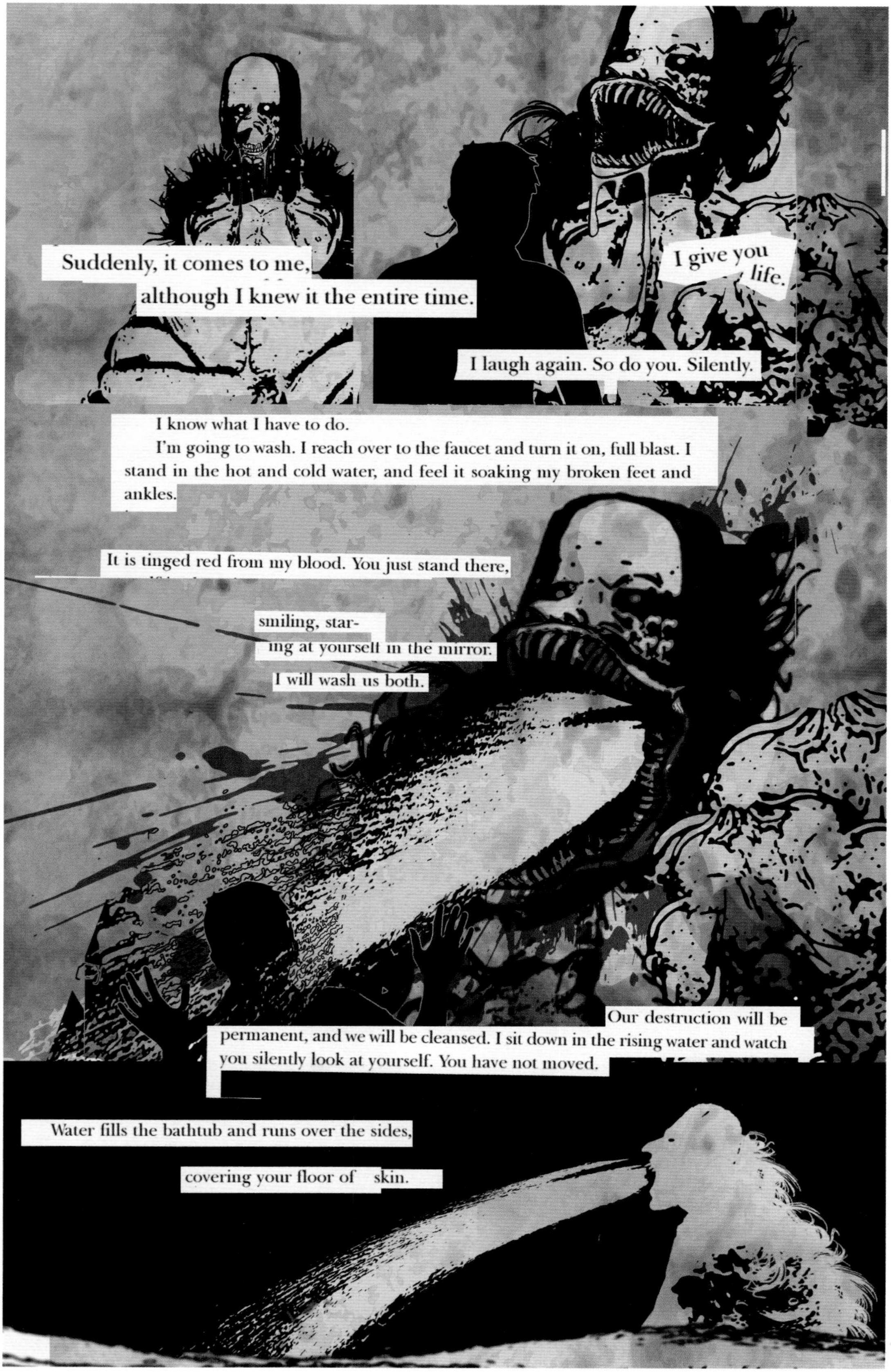

Suddenly, it comes to me,
although I knew it the entire time.
I give you life.
I laugh again. So do you. Silently.
I know what I have to do.
I'm going to wash. I reach over to the faucet and turn it on, full blast. I stand in the hot and cold water, and feel it soaking my broken feet and ankles.
It is tinged red from my blood. You just stand there,
smiling, star-
ing at yourself in the mirror.
I will wash us both.
Our destruction will be
permanent, and we will be cleansed. I sit down in the rising water and watch you silently look at yourself. You have not moved.
Water fills the bathtub and runs over the sides,
covering your floor of skin.

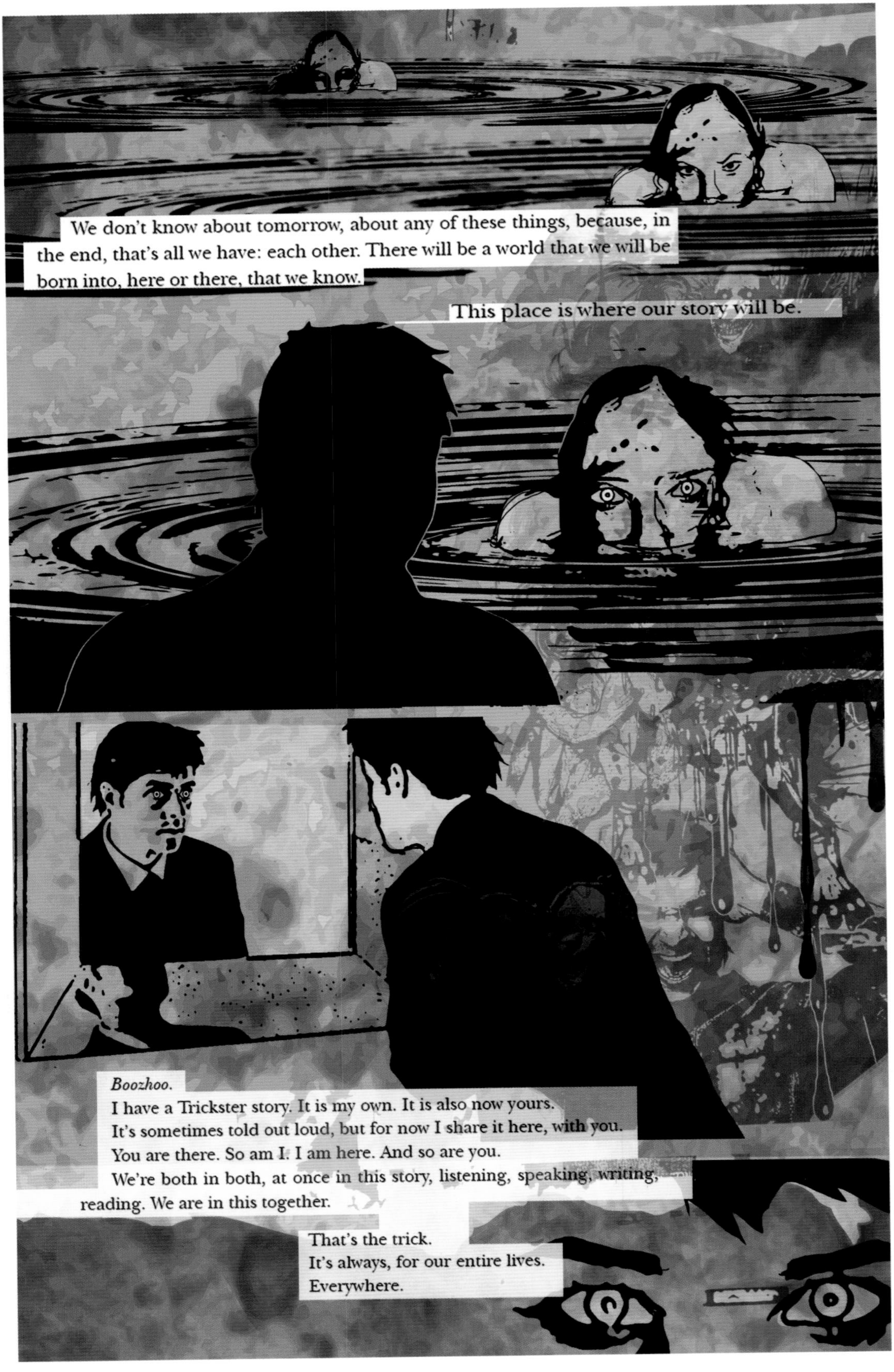
We don't know about tomorrow, about any of these things, because, in the end, that's all we have: each other. There will be a world that we will be born into, here or there, that we know.
This place is where our story will be.
Boozhoo.
I have a Trickster story. It is my own. It is also now yours.
It's sometimes told out loud, but for now I share it here, with you.
You are there. So am I. I am here. And so are you.
We're both in both, at once in this story, listening, speaking, writing, reading. We are in this together.
That's the trick.
It's always, for our entire lives.
Everywhere.

The Strange People

Louise Erdrich

ILLUSTRATION & COLORS: Elizabeth LaPensée

Louise Erdrich—an enrolled member of the Turtle Mountain Band of Chippewa Indians, a band of the Anishinaabe—is the author of *Love Medicine* and *LaRose* and is widely acclaimed as one of the most significant writers of the second wave of the Native American Renaissance. In 2009 her novel *The Plague of Doves* was a finalist for the Pulitzer Prize for Fiction and also received an Anisfield-Wolf Book Award. In 2012 she received the National Book Award for Fiction for her novel *The Round House.* In 2015 she was awarded the Library of Congress Prize for American Fiction.

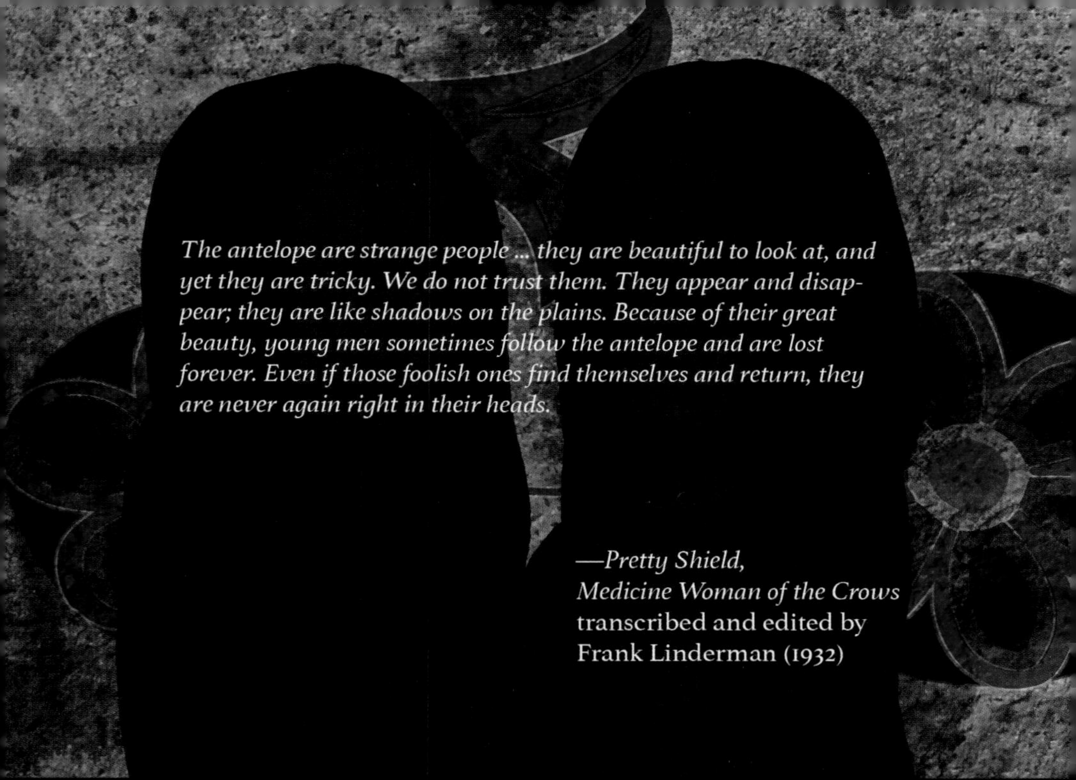
The antelope are strange people ... they are beautiful to look at, and yet they are tricky. We do not trust them. They appear and disappear; they are like shadows on the plains. Because of their great beauty, young men sometimes follow the antelope and are lost forever. Even if those foolish ones find themselves and return, they are never again right in their heads.
—*Pretty Shield,*
Medicine Woman of the Crows
transcribed and edited by
Frank Linderman (1932)

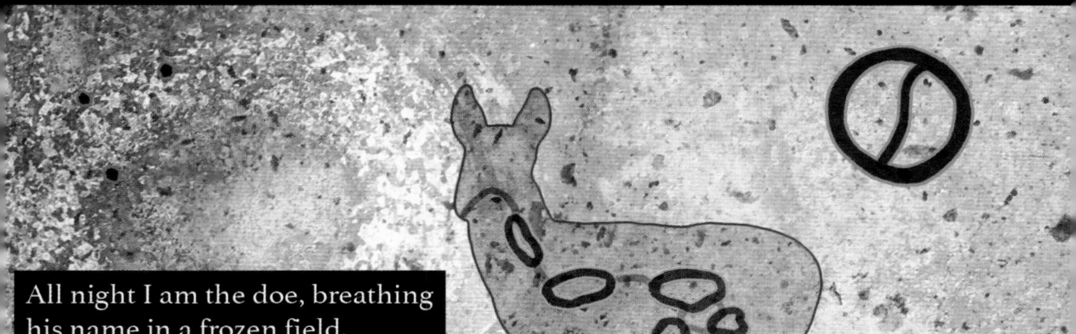
All night I am the doe, breathing
his name in a frozen field,
the small mist of the word
drifting always before me.

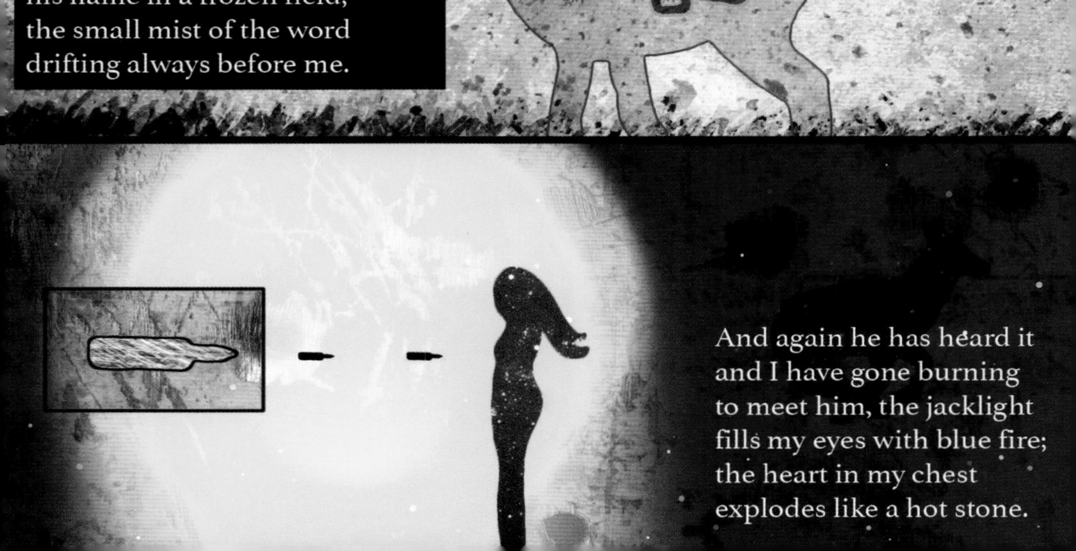
And again he has heard it
and I have gone burning
to meet him, the jacklight
fills my eyes with blue fire;
the heart in my chest
explodes like a hot stone.

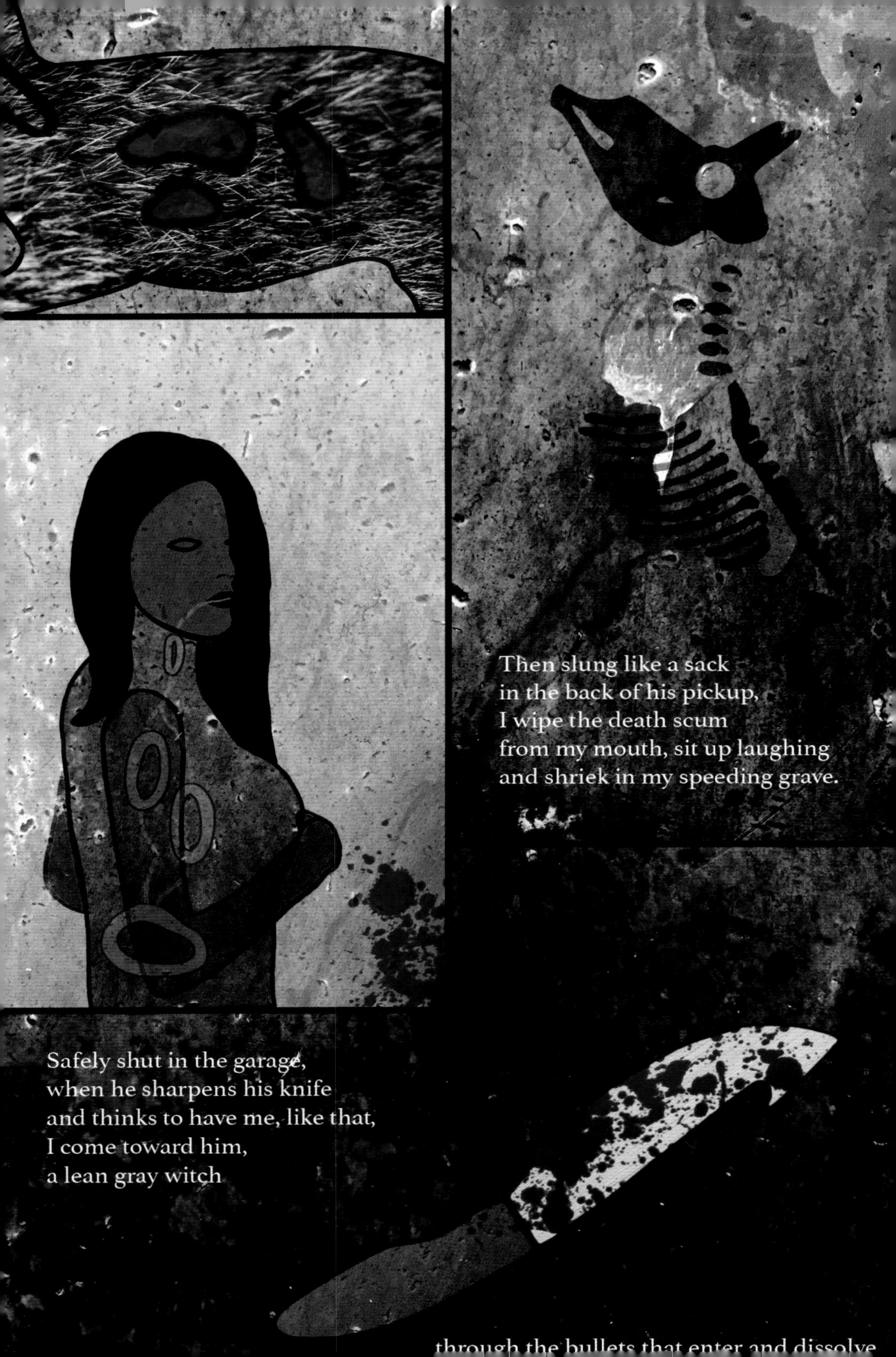
Then slung like a sack
in the back of his pickup,
I wipe the death scum
from my mouth, sit up laughing
and shriek in my speeding grave.
Safely shut in the garage,
when he sharpens his knife
and thinks to have me, like that,
I come toward him,
a lean gray witch
through the bullets that enter and dissolve

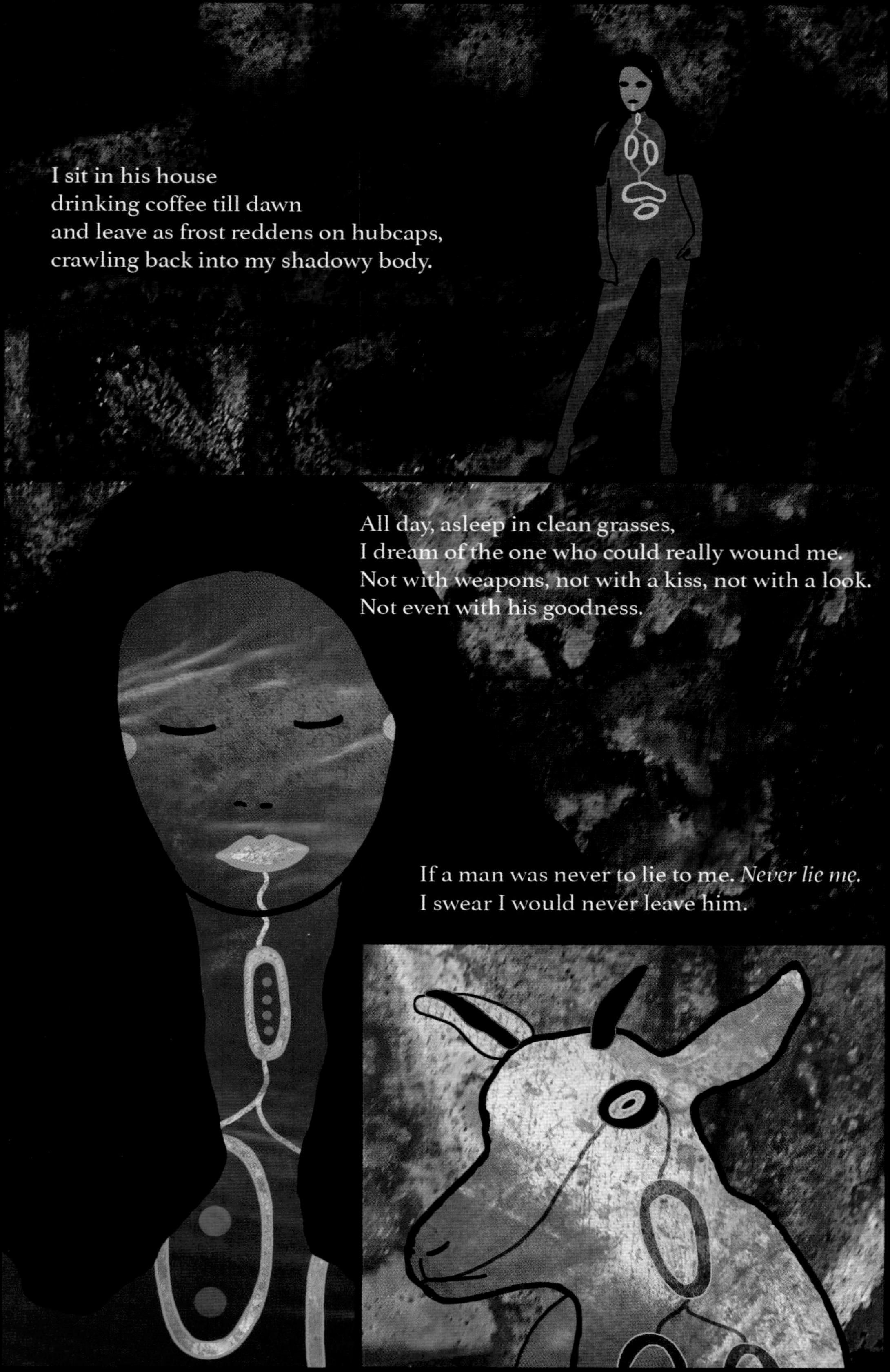
I sit in his house
drinking coffee till dawn
and leave as frost reddens on hubcaps,
crawling back into my shadowy body.
All day, asleep in clean grasses,
I dream of the one who could really wound me.
Not with weapons, not with a kiss, not with a look.
Not even with his goodness.
If a man was never to lie to me. *Never lie me.*
I swear I would never leave him.

Deer Dancer

Joy Harjo

ILLUSTRATION & COLORS: Weshoyot Alvitre

Joy Harjo is a member of the Mvskoke Nation and an award-winning musician and performance artist. She has received a Rasmusson US Artists Fellowship and is a founding board member of the Native Arts and Cultures Foundation. Her seven books of poetry, which include such well-known titles as *How We Became Human*, *The Woman Who Fell from the Sky*, and *She Had Some Horses*, have garnered many awards, including the New Mexico Governor's Award for Excellence in the Arts, the Lifetime Achievement Award from the Native Writers Circle of the Americas, and the William Carlos Williams Award from the Poetry Society of America. She released *For a Girl Becoming,* a young adult/coming-of-age book, in 2009.

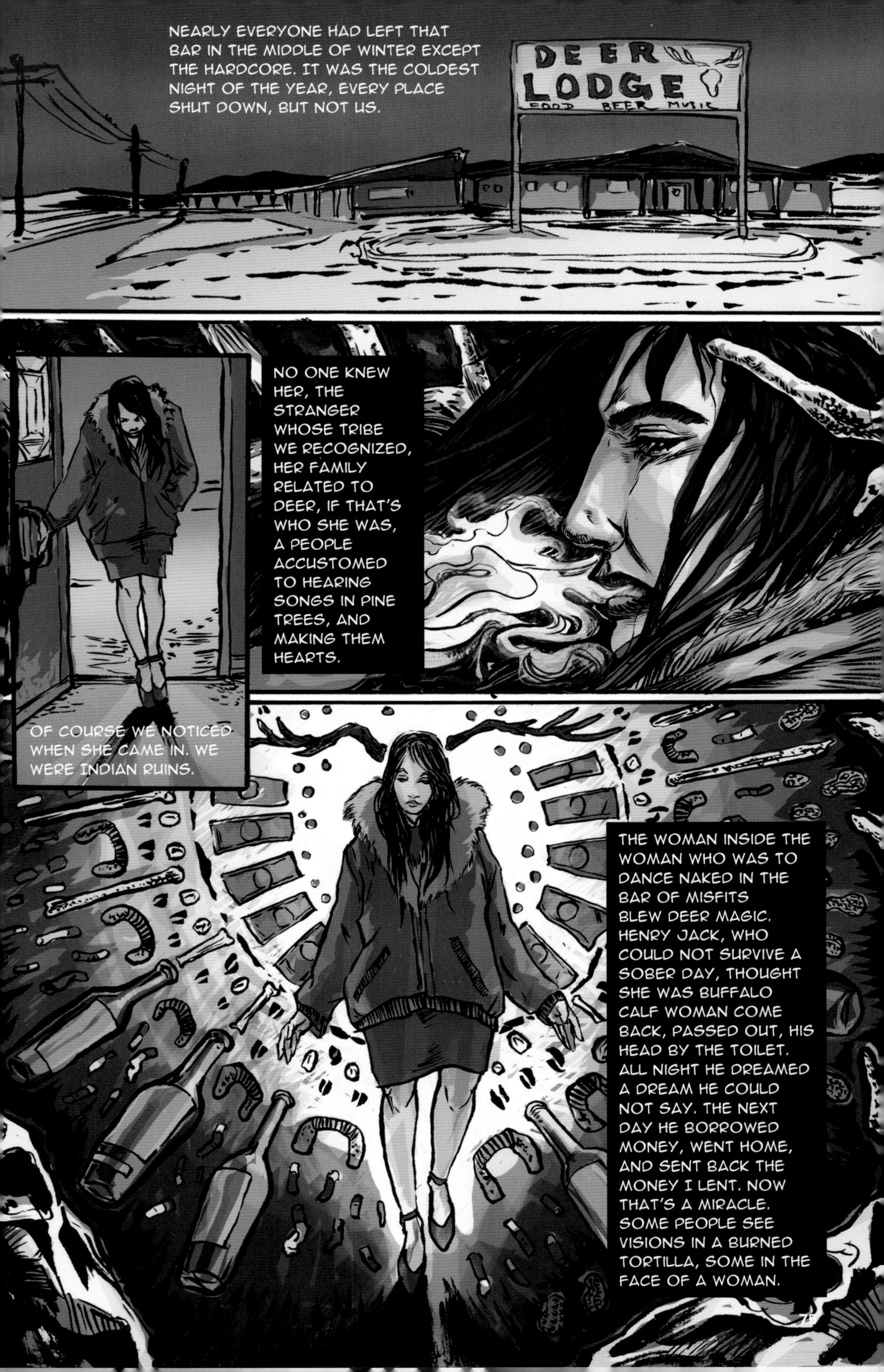
NEARLY EVERYONE HAD LEFT THAT BAR IN THE MIDDLE OF WINTER EXCEPT THE HARDCORE. IT WAS THE COLDEST NIGHT OF THE YEAR, EVERY PLACE SHUT DOWN, BUT NOT US.
DEER LODGE
FOOD BEER MUSIC
OF COURSE WE NOTICED WHEN SHE CAME IN. WE WERE INDIAN RUINS.
NO ONE KNEW HER, THE STRANGER WHOSE TRIBE WE RECOGNIZED, HER FAMILY RELATED TO DEER, IF THAT'S WHO SHE WAS, A PEOPLE ACCUSTOMED TO HEARING SONGS IN PINE TREES, AND MAKING THEM HEARTS.
THE WOMAN INSIDE THE WOMAN WHO WAS TO DANCE NAKED IN THE BAR OF MISFITS BLEW DEER MAGIC. HENRY JACK, WHO COULD NOT SURVIVE A SOBER DAY, THOUGHT SHE WAS BUFFALO CALF WOMAN COME BACK, PASSED OUT, HIS HEAD BY THE TOILET. ALL NIGHT HE DREAMED A DREAM HE COULD NOT SAY. THE NEXT DAY HE BORROWED MONEY, WENT HOME, AND SENT BACK THE MONEY I LENT. NOW THAT'S A MIRACLE. SOME PEOPLE SEE VISIONS IN A BURNED TORTILLA, SOME IN THE FACE OF A WOMAN.

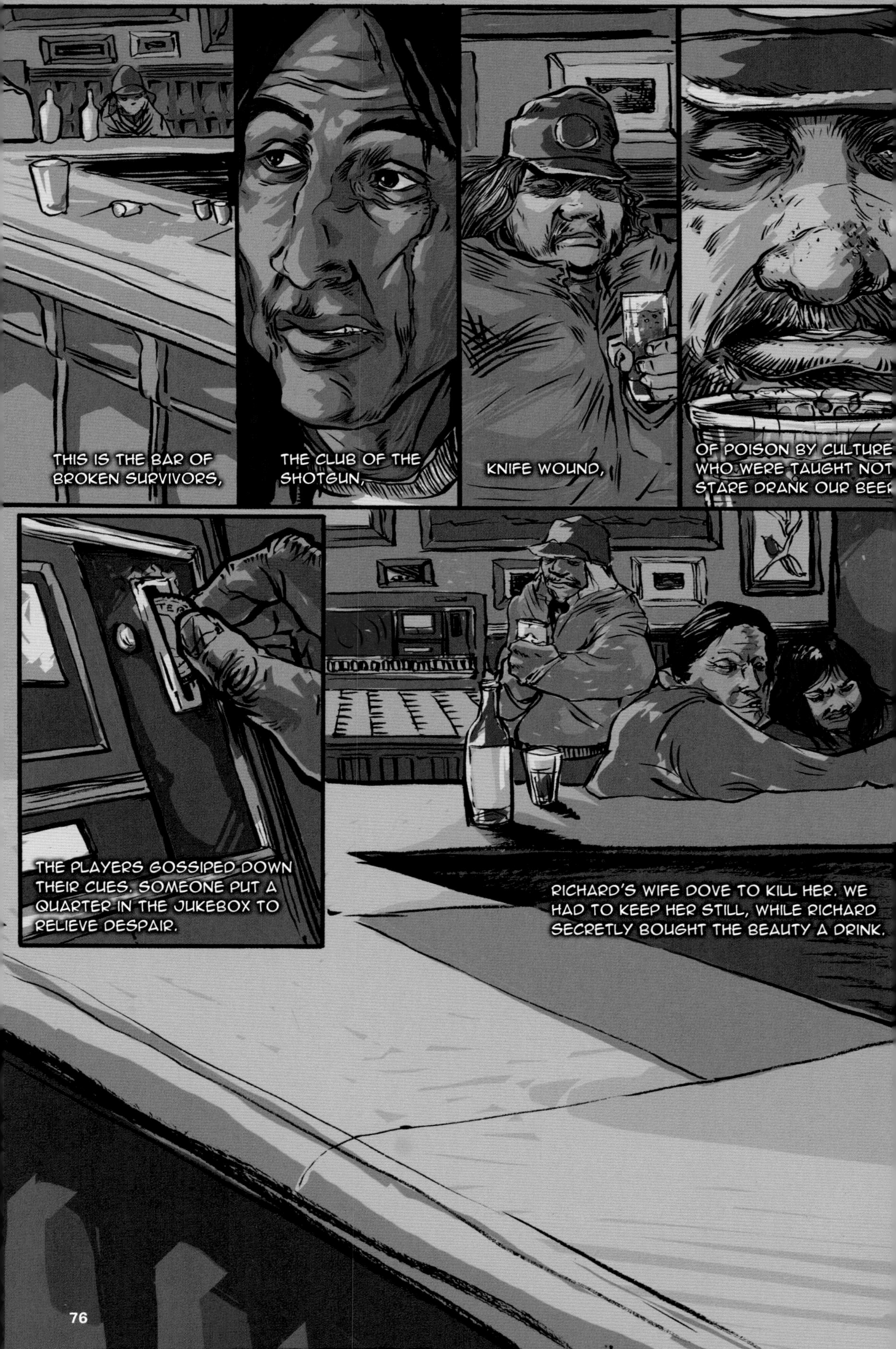
THIS IS THE BAR OF BROKEN SURVIVORS,
THE CLUB OF THE SHOTGUN,
KNIFE WOUND,
OF POISON BY CULTURE WHO WERE TAUGHT NOT STARE DRANK OUR BEER
THE PLAYERS GOSSIPED DOWN THEIR CUES. SOMEONE PUT A QUARTER IN THE JUKEBOX TO RELIEVE DESPAIR.
RICHARD'S WIFE DOVE TO KILL HER. WE HAD TO KEEP HER STILL, WHILE RICHARD SECRETLY BOUGHT THE BEAUTY A DRINK.

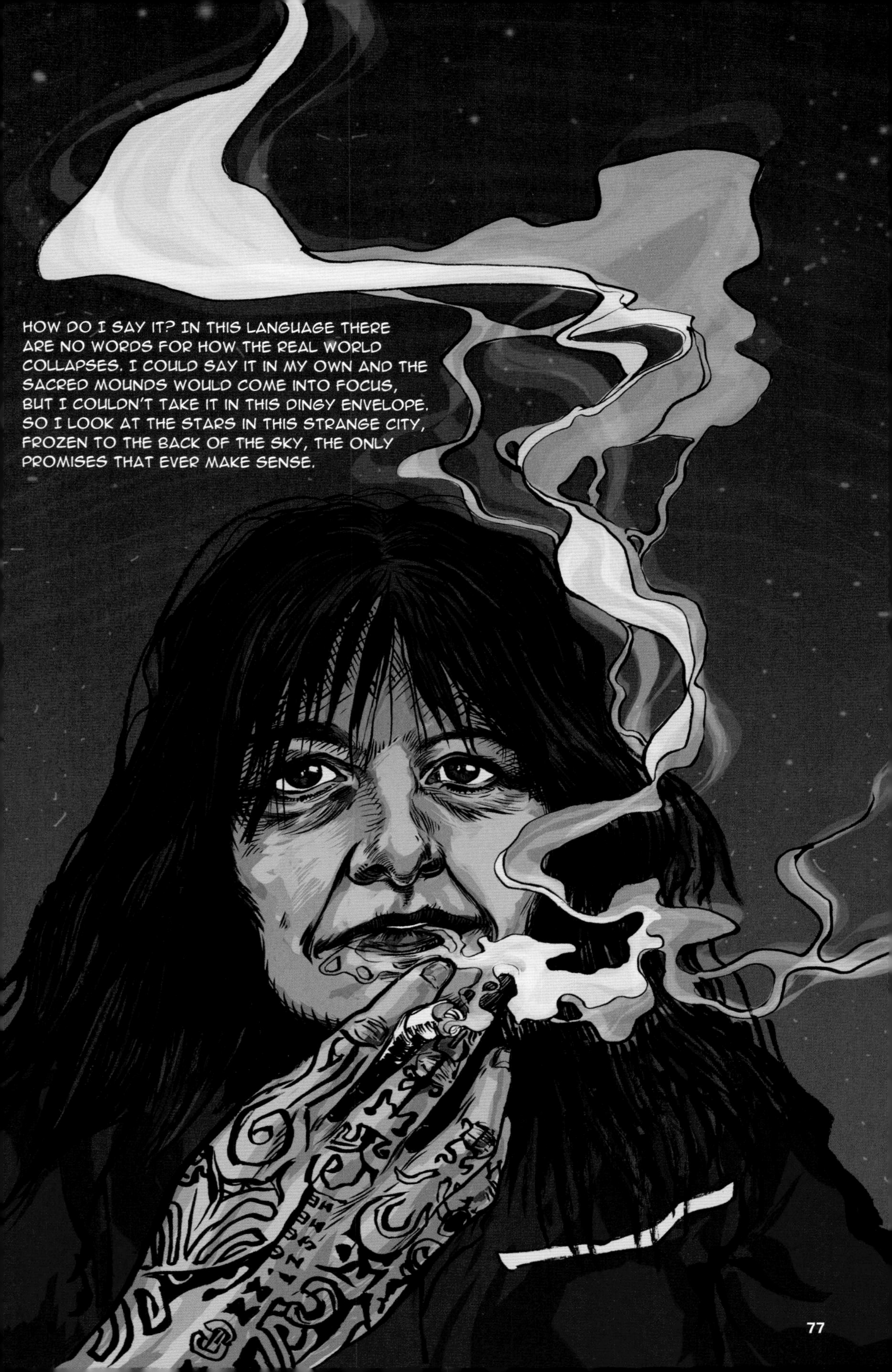
HOW DO I SAY IT? IN THIS LANGUAGE THERE ARE NO WORDS FOR HOW THE REAL WORLD COLLAPSES. I COULD SAY IT IN MY OWN AND THE SACRED MOUNDS WOULD COME INTO FOCUS, BUT I COULDN'T TAKE IT IN THIS DINGY ENVELOPE. SO I LOOK AT THE STARS IN THIS STRANGE CITY, FROZEN TO THE BACK OF THE SKY, THE ONLY PROMISES THAT EVER MAKE SENSE.

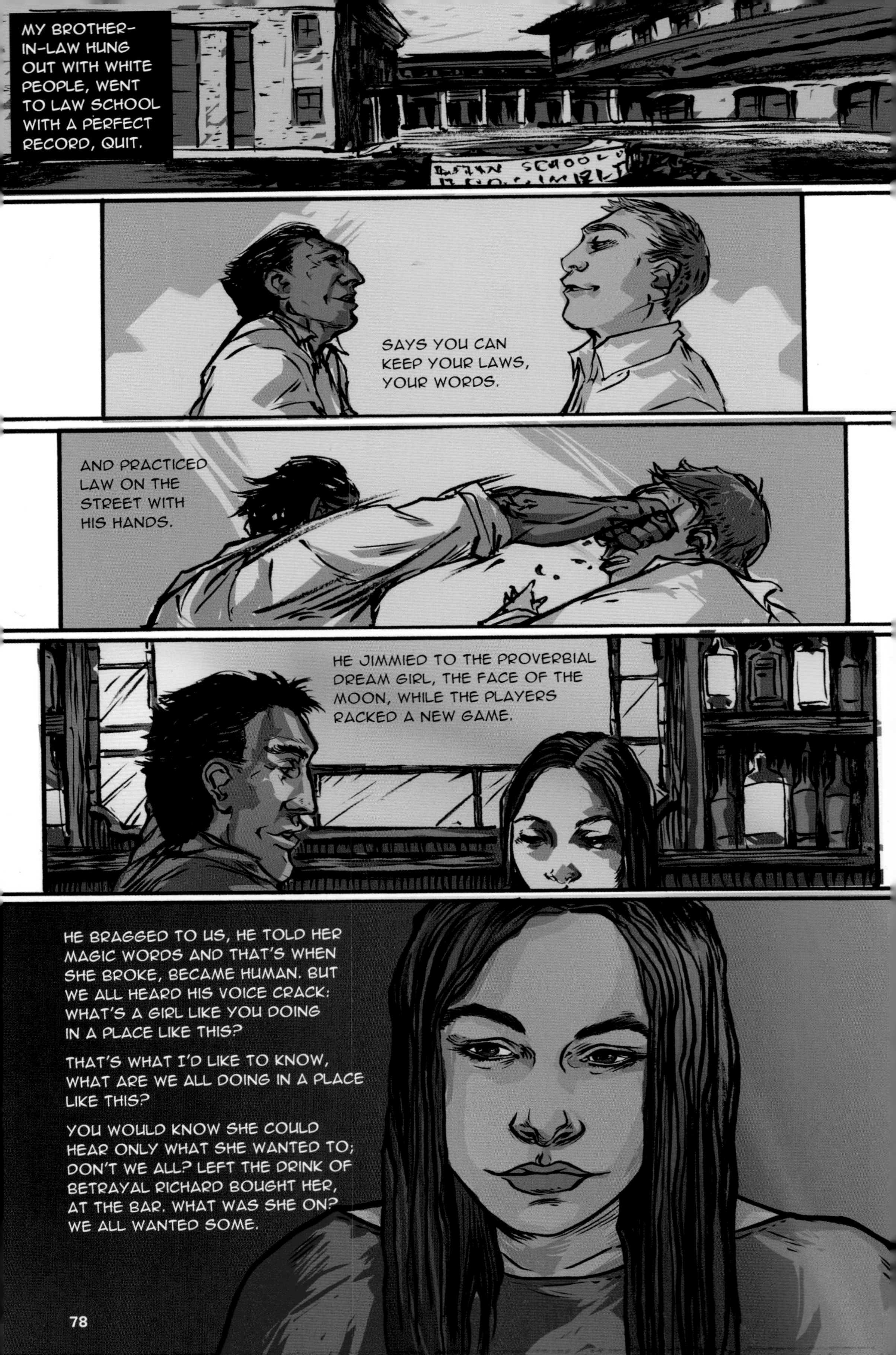
MY BROTHER-IN-LAW HUNG OUT WITH WHITE PEOPLE, WENT TO LAW SCHOOL WITH A PERFECT RECORD, QUIT.
SAYS YOU CAN KEEP YOUR LAWS, YOUR WORDS.
AND PRACTICED LAW ON THE STREET WITH HIS HANDS.
HE JIMMIED TO THE PROVERBIAL DREAM GIRL, THE FACE OF THE MOON, WHILE THE PLAYERS RACKED A NEW GAME.
HE BRAGGED TO US, HE TOLD HER MAGIC WORDS AND THAT'S WHEN SHE BROKE, BECAME HUMAN. BUT WE ALL HEARD HIS VOICE CRACK: WHAT'S A GIRL LIKE YOU DOING IN A PLACE LIKE THIS?
THAT'S WHAT I'D LIKE TO KNOW, WHAT ARE WE ALL DOING IN A PLACE LIKE THIS?
YOU WOULD KNOW SHE COULD HEAR ONLY WHAT SHE WANTED TO; DON'T WE ALL? LEFT THE DRINK OF BETRAYAL RICHARD BOUGHT HER, AT THE BAR. WHAT WAS SHE ON? WE ALL WANTED SOME.

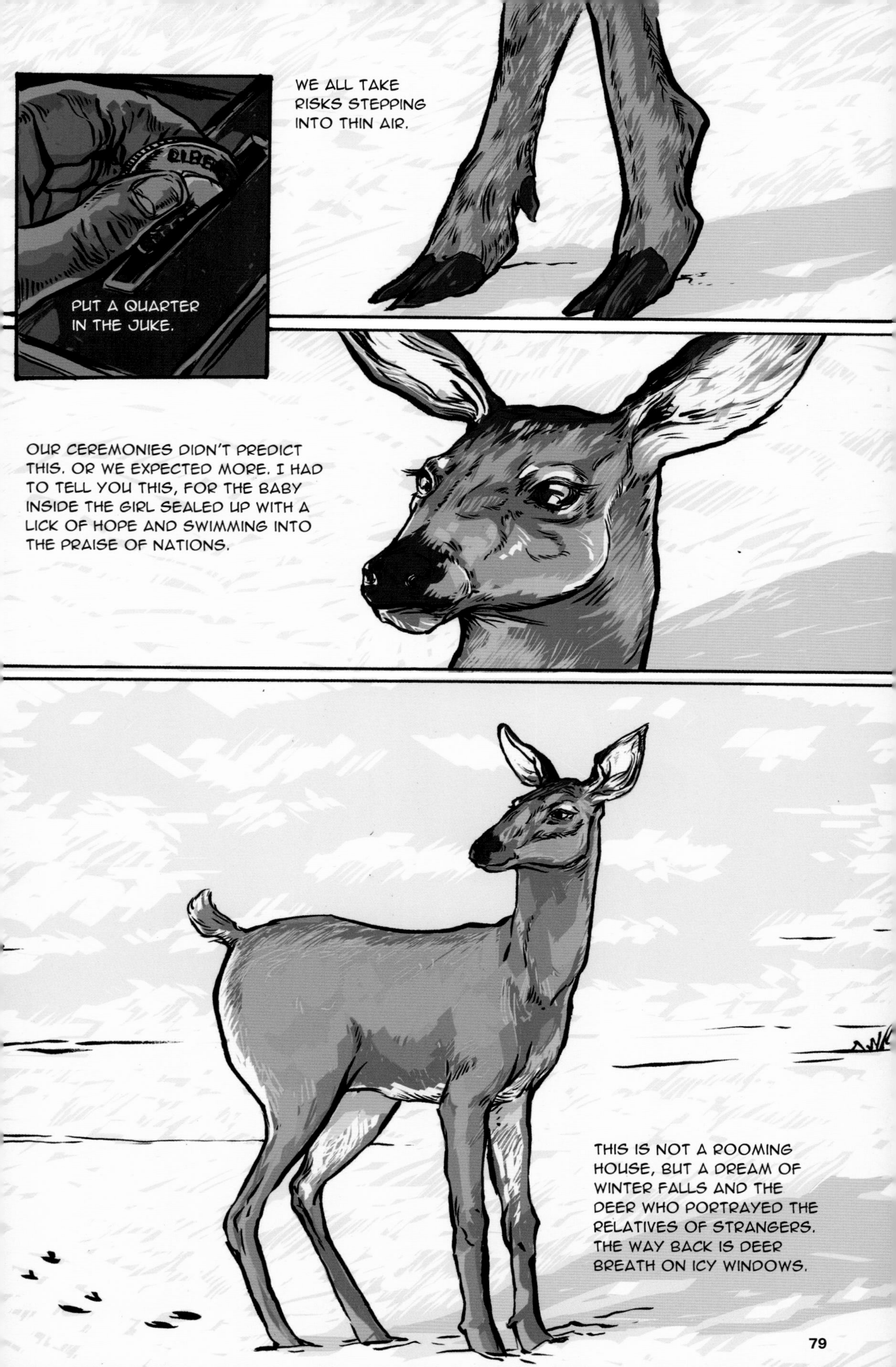
PUT A QUARTER IN THE JUKE.
WE ALL TAKE RISKS STEPPING INTO THIN AIR.
OUR CEREMONIES DIDN'T PREDICT THIS. OR WE EXPECTED MORE. I HAD TO TELL YOU THIS, FOR THE BABY INSIDE THE GIRL SEALED UP WITH A LICK OF HOPE AND SWIMMING INTO THE PRAISE OF NATIONS.
THIS IS NOT A ROOMING HOUSE, BUT A DREAM OF WINTER FALLS AND THE DEER WHO PORTRAYED THE RELATIVES OF STRANGERS. THE WAY BACK IS DEER BREATH ON ICY WINDOWS.

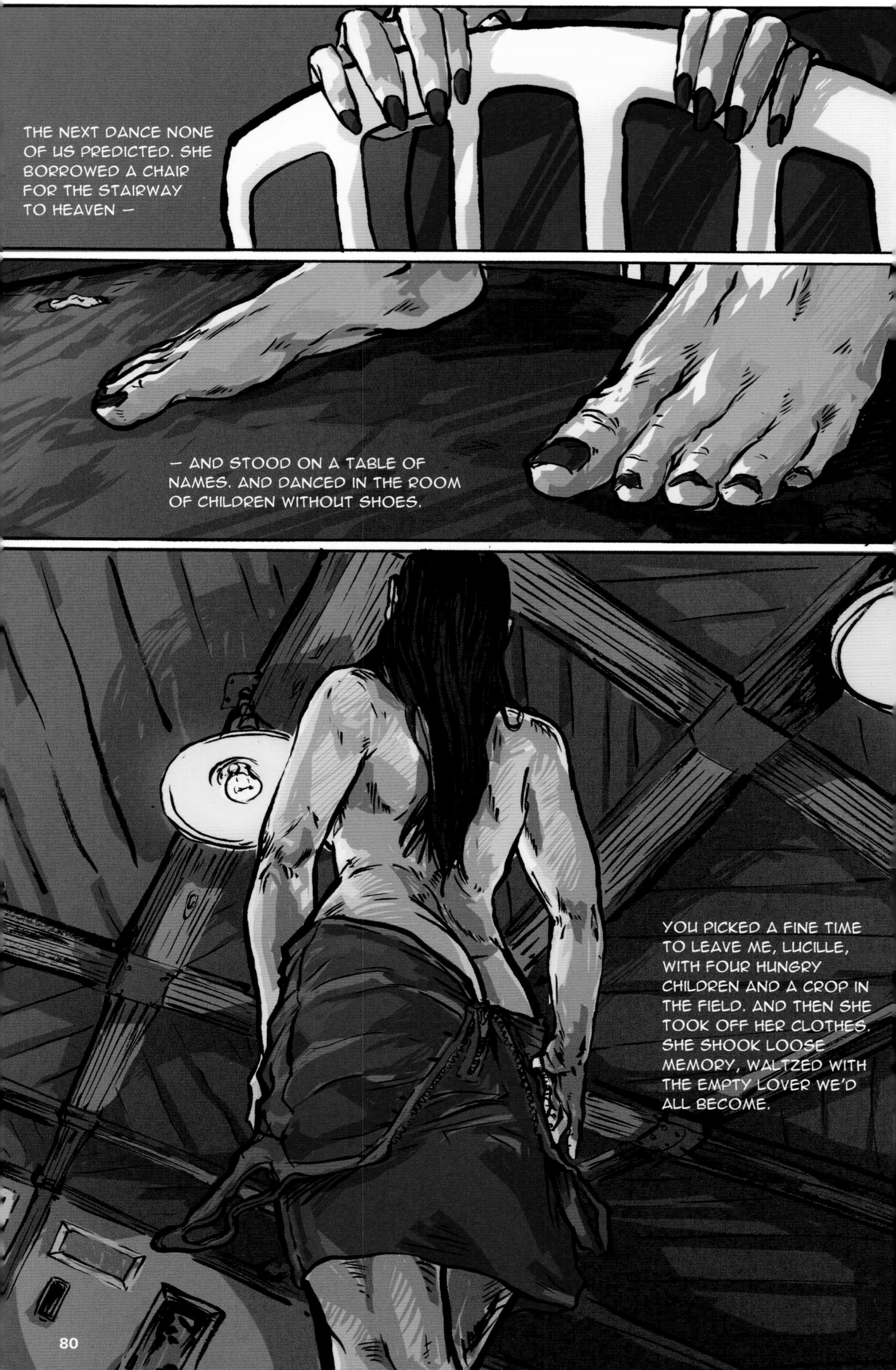
THE NEXT DANCE NONE OF US PREDICTED. SHE BORROWED A CHAIR FOR THE STAIRWAY TO HEAVEN —
— AND STOOD ON A TABLE OF NAMES. AND DANCED IN THE ROOM OF CHILDREN WITHOUT SHOES.
YOU PICKED A FINE TIME TO LEAVE ME, LUCILLE, WITH FOUR HUNGRY CHILDREN AND A CROP IN THE FIELD. AND THEN SHE TOOK OFF HER CLOTHES. SHE SHOOK LOOSE MEMORY, WALTZED WITH THE EMPTY LOVER WE'D ALL BECOME.

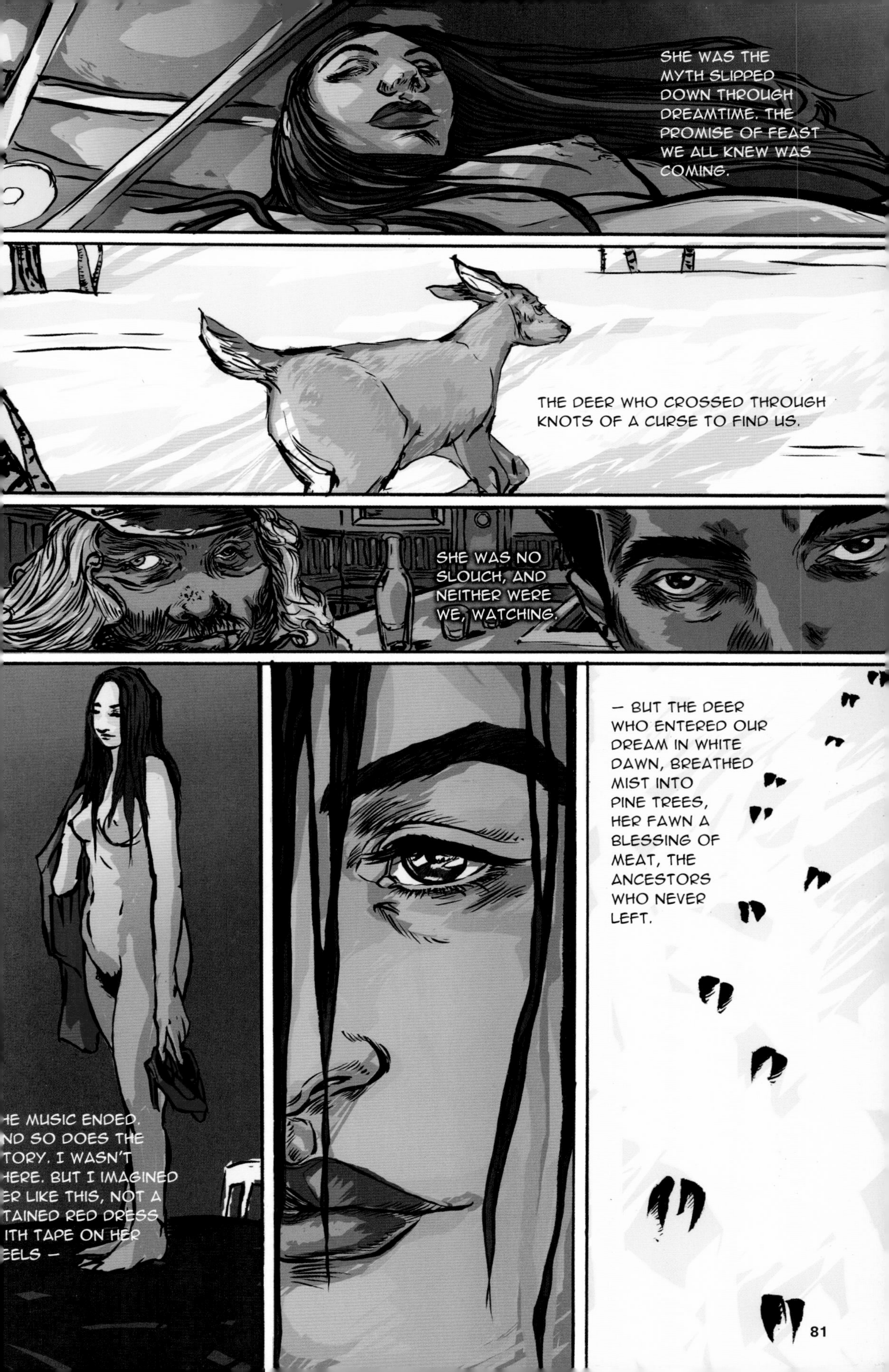
SHE WAS THE MYTH SLIPPED DOWN THROUGH DREAMTIME. THE PROMISE OF FEAST WE ALL KNEW WAS COMING.
THE DEER WHO CROSSED THROUGH KNOTS OF A CURSE TO FIND US.
SHE WAS NO SLOUCH, AND NEITHER WERE WE, WATCHING.
HE MUSIC ENDED. ND SO DOES THE TORY. I WASN'T HERE. BUT I IMAGINED ER LIKE THIS, NOT A TAINED RED DRESS ITH TAPE ON HER EELS —
— BUT THE DEER WHO ENTERED OUR DREAM IN WHITE DAWN, BREATHED MIST INTO PINE TREES, HER FAWN A BLESSING OF MEAT, THE ANCESTORS WHO NEVER LEFT.

Mermaids

Richard Van Camp

ILLUSTRATION: Scott B. Henderson
COLORS: Donovan Yaciuk

Richard Van Camp is a proud member of the Tłįcho Dene from Fort Smith, Northwest Territories. He is the author of two children's books with the Cree artist George Littlechild: *A Man Called Raven* and *What's the Most Beautiful Thing You Know About Horses?* His novel *The Lesser Blessed* is now a feature film with First Generation Films; his collections of short fiction include *Angel Wing Splash Pattern*, *The Moon of Letting Go and Other Stories*, *Godless but Loyal to Heaven*, and *Night Moves*. He is the author of four baby books: *Welcome Song for Baby: A Lullaby for Newborns*, *Nighty-Night: A Bedtime Song for Babies*, *Little You* (now translated into Cree, Dene, and South Slavey), and *We Sang You Home*, and he has two comic books out with the Healthy Aboriginal Network: *Kiss Me Deadly* and *Path of the Warrior*. His graphic novel *Three Feathers* is about restorative justice; his novel, *Whistle*, is about mental health and asking for forgiveness; and his graphic novel *The Blue Raven* is about mental health and the power of culture and friends. His Eisner-nominated graphic novel *A Blanket of Butterflies* is about peacemaking, where a grandmother is the hero of the story, and his graphic novel, *Spirit*, is about suicide prevention. Cinematic adaptations of his work include "Mohawk Midnight Runners," by Zoe Hopkins, based on Richard's short story "Dogrib Midnight Runners," from *The Moon of Letting Go*; Kelvin Redver's adaptation of "firebear called them faith healers"; Jay Cardinal Villeneuve's adaptation of "Hickey Gone Wrong," based on Richard's comic book with Chris Auchter; and "Three Feathers," which is available for viewing in Bush Cree, Dene, and South Slavey, as well as English, based on his graphic novel. You can visit Richard on Facebook, Twitter, and at www.richardvancamp.com.

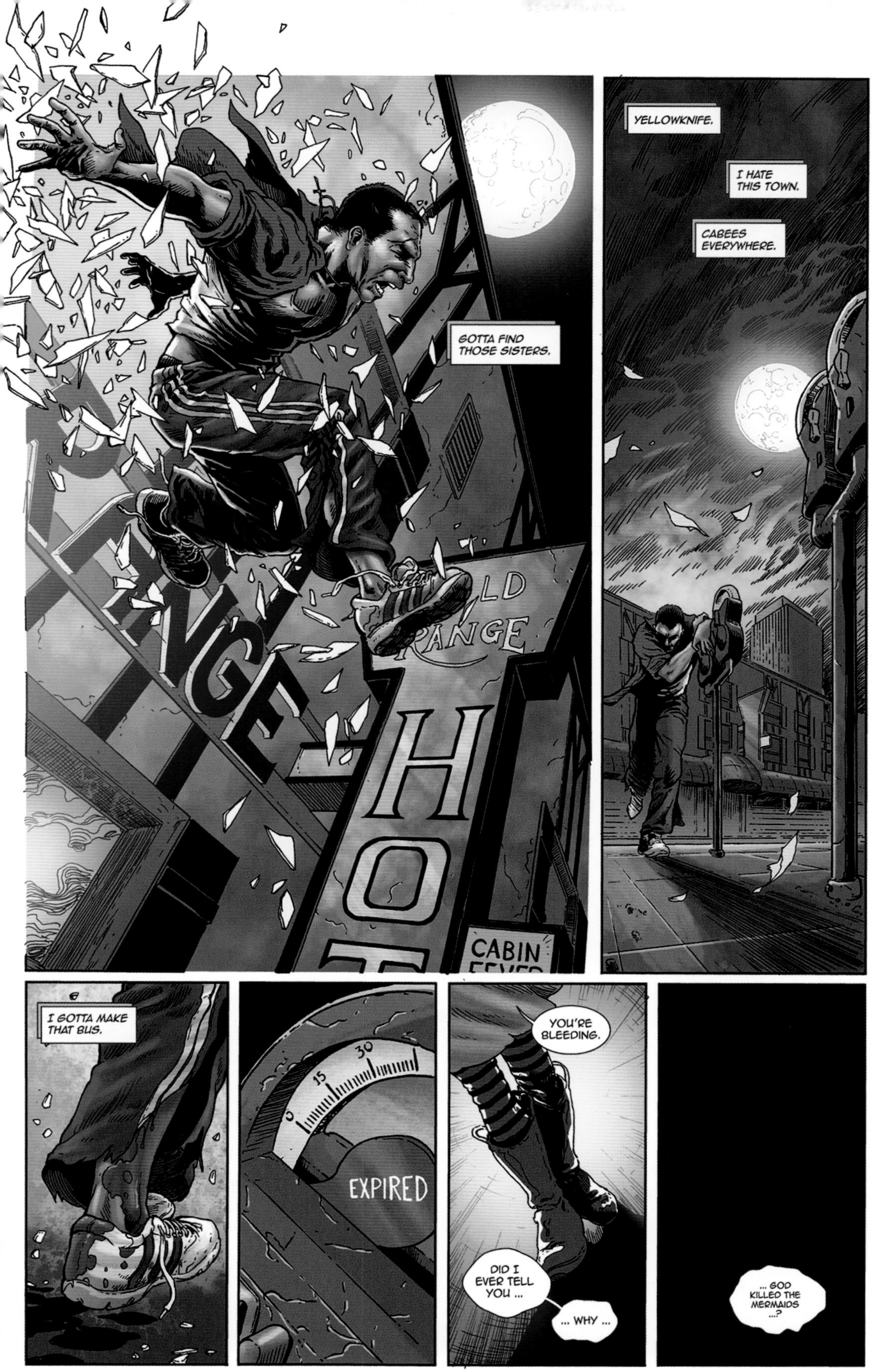
GOTTA FIND THOSE SISTERS.
OLD RANGE
HOT
CABIN FEVER
YELLOWKNIFE.
I HATE THIS TOWN.
CABEES EVERYWHERE.
I GOTTA MAKE THAT BUS.
0
15
30
EXPIRED
YOU'RE BLEEDING.
DID I EVER TELL YOU ...
... WHY ...
... GOD KILLED THE MERMAIDS ...?

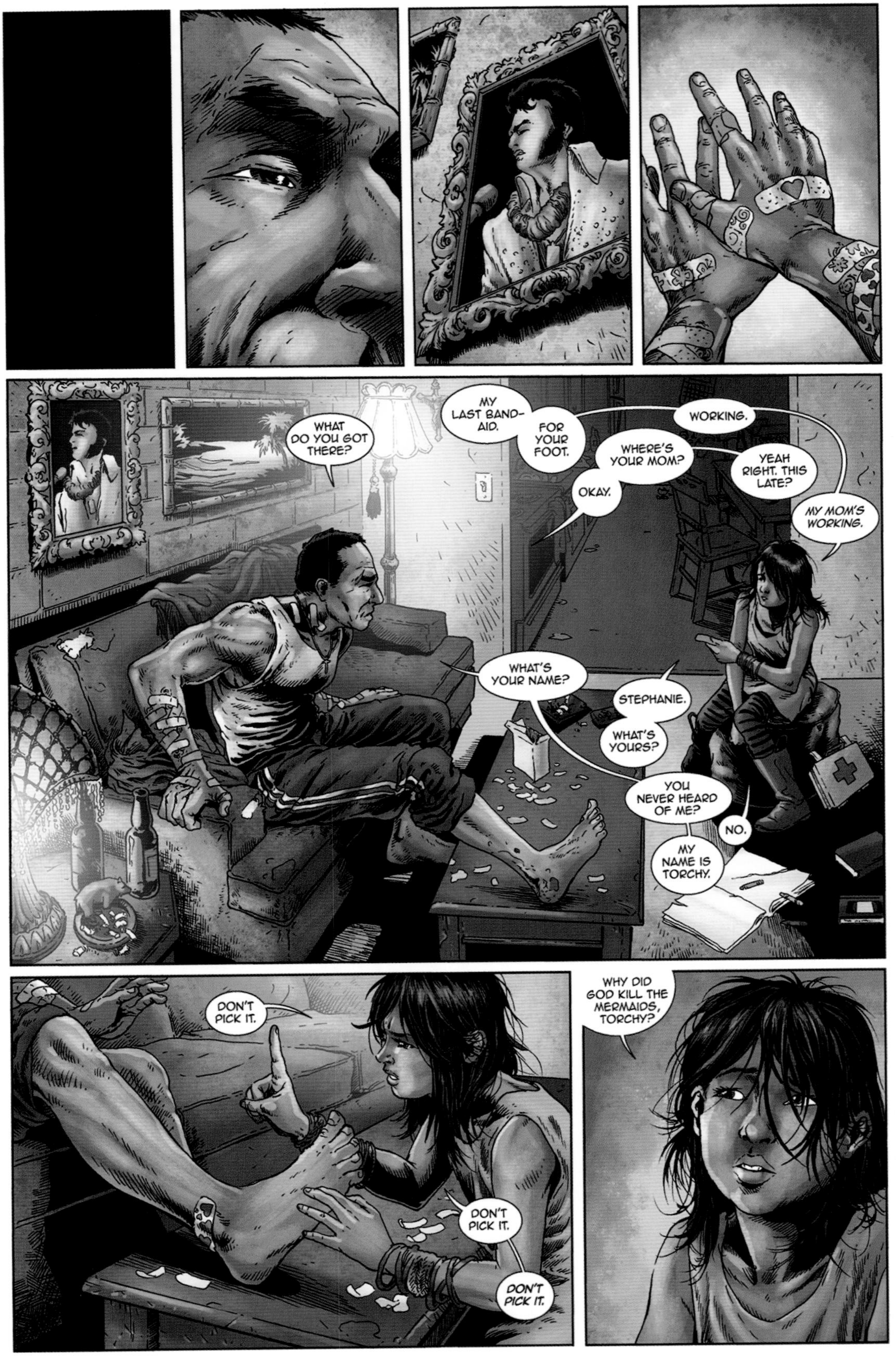
WHAT DO YOU GOT THERE?
MY LAST BAND-AID.
FOR YOUR FOOT.
OKAY.
WHERE'S YOUR MOM?
MY MOM'S WORKING.
WORKING.
YEAH RIGHT. THIS LATE?
WHAT'S YOUR NAME?
STEPHANIE.
WHAT'S YOURS?
YOU NEVER HEARD OF ME?
NO.
MY NAME IS TORCHY.
DON'T PICK IT.
DON'T PICK IT.
DON'T PICK IT.
WHY DID GOD KILL THE MERMAIDS, TORCHY?

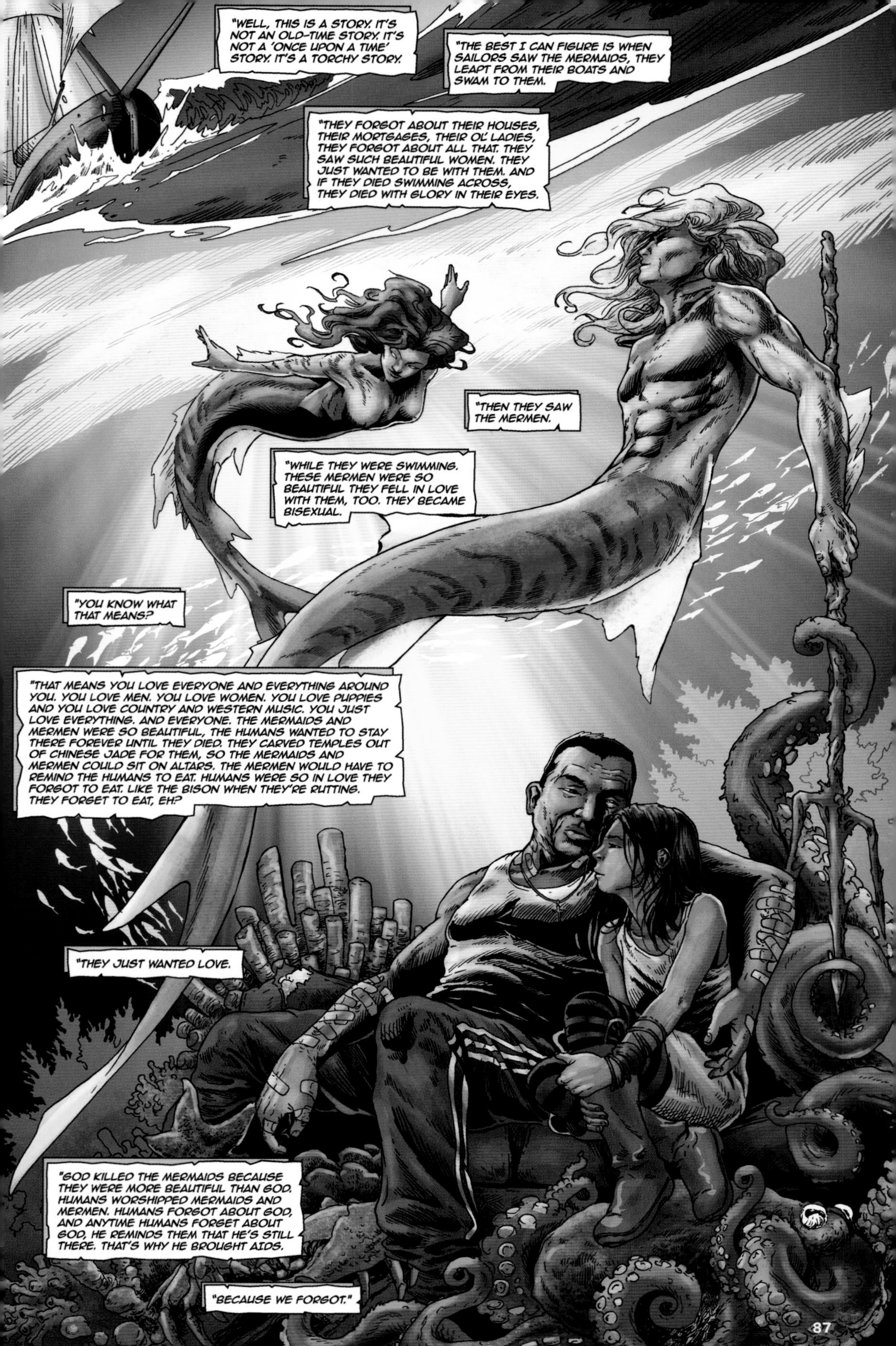
"WELL, THIS IS A STORY. IT'S NOT AN OLD-TIME STORY. IT'S NOT A 'ONCE UPON A TIME' STORY. IT'S A TORCHY STORY.
"THE BEST I CAN FIGURE IS WHEN SAILORS SAW THE MERMAIDS, THEY LEAPT FROM THEIR BOATS AND SWAM TO THEM.
"THEY FORGOT ABOUT THEIR HOUSES, THEIR MORTGAGES, THEIR OL' LADIES, THEY FORGOT ABOUT ALL THAT. THEY SAW SUCH BEAUTIFUL WOMEN. THEY JUST WANTED TO BE WITH THEM. AND IF THEY DIED SWIMMING ACROSS, THEY DIED WITH GLORY IN THEIR EYES.
"THEN THEY SAW THE MERMEN.
"WHILE THEY WERE SWIMMING. THESE MERMEN WERE SO BEAUTIFUL THEY FELL IN LOVE WITH THEM, TOO. THEY BECAME BISEXUAL.
"YOU KNOW WHAT THAT MEANS?
"THAT MEANS YOU LOVE EVERYONE AND EVERYTHING AROUND YOU. YOU LOVE MEN. YOU LOVE WOMEN. YOU LOVE PUPPIES AND YOU LOVE COUNTRY AND WESTERN MUSIC. YOU JUST LOVE EVERYTHING. AND EVERYONE. THE MERMAIDS AND MERMEN WERE SO BEAUTIFUL, THE HUMANS WANTED TO STAY THERE FOREVER UNTIL THEY DIED. THEY CARVED TEMPLES OUT OF CHINESE JADE FOR THEM, SO THE MERMAIDS AND MERMEN COULD SIT ON ALTARS. THE MERMEN WOULD HAVE TO REMIND THE HUMANS TO EAT. HUMANS WERE SO IN LOVE THEY FORGOT TO EAT. LIKE THE BISON WHEN THEY'RE RUTTING. THEY FORGET TO EAT, EH?
"THEY JUST WANTED LOVE.
"GOD KILLED THE MERMAIDS BECAUSE THEY WERE MORE BEAUTIFUL THAN GOD. HUMANS WORSHIPPED MERMAIDS AND MERMEN. HUMANS FORGOT ABOUT GOD, AND ANYTIME HUMANS FORGET ABOUT GOD, HE REMINDS THEM THAT HE'S STILL THERE. THAT'S WHY HE BROUGHT AIDS.
"BECAUSE WE FORGOT."

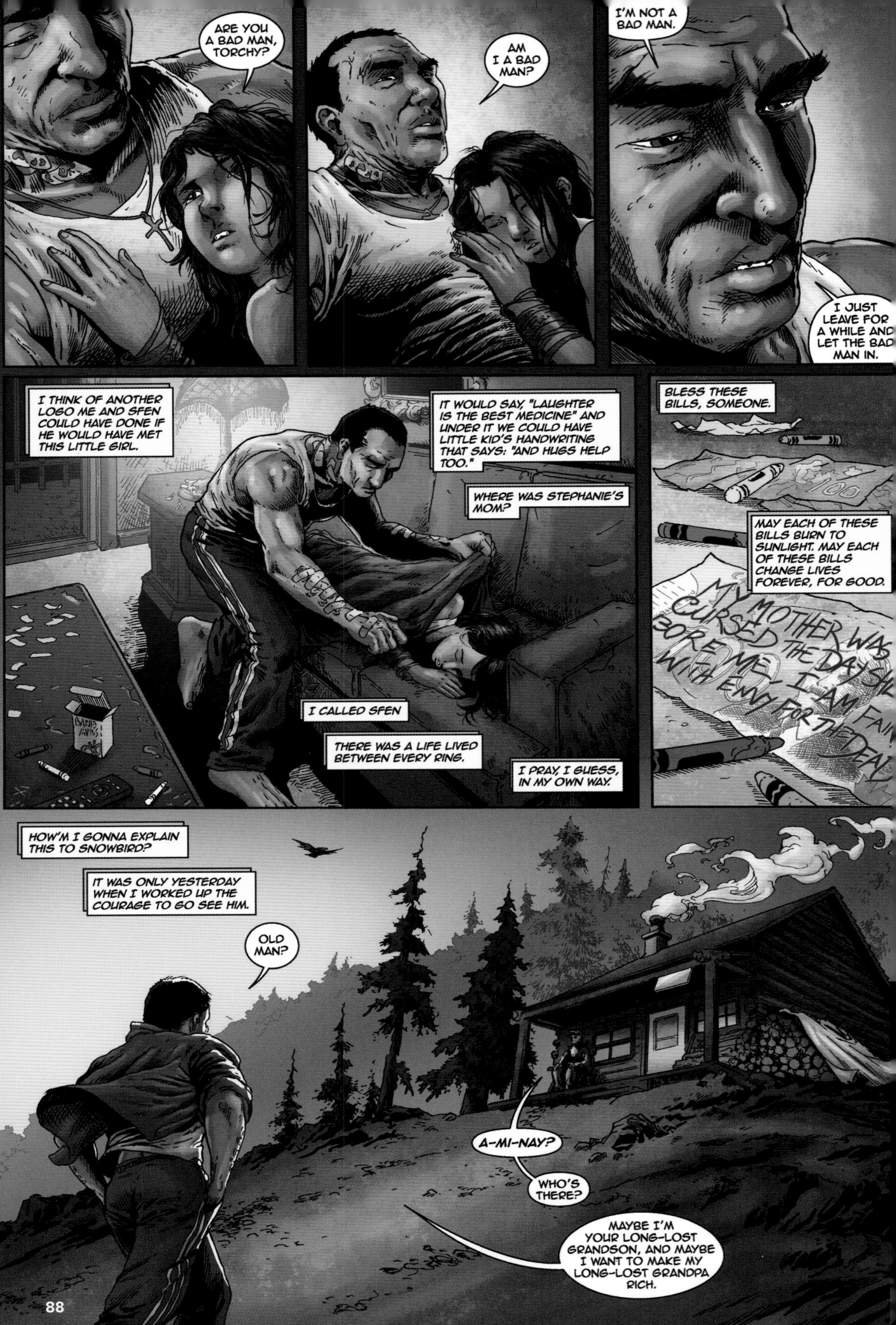

ARE YOU A BAD MAN, TORCHY?
AM I A BAD MAN?
I'M NOT A BAD MAN.
I JUST LEAVE FOR A WHILE AND LET THE BAD MAN IN.
I THINK OF ANOTHER LOGO ME AND SFEN COULD HAVE DONE IF HE WOULD HAVE MET THIS LITTLE GIRL.
IT WOULD SAY, "LAUGHTER IS THE BEST MEDICINE" AND UNDER IT WE COULD HAVE LITTLE KID'S HANDWRITING THAT SAYS: "AND HUGS HELP TOO."
WHERE WAS STEPHANIE'S MOM?
I CALLED SFEN
THERE WAS A LIFE LIVED BETWEEN EVERY RING.
I PRAY, I GUESS, IN MY OWN WAY.
BLESS THESE BILLS, SOMEONE.
MAY EACH OF THESE BILLS BURN TO SUNLIGHT. MAY EACH OF THESE BILLS CHANGE LIVES FOREVER, FOR GOOD.
MY MOTHER WAS CURSED THE DAY SH BORE ME, I AM FAIN WITH ENVY FOR THE DEA
HOW'M I GONNA EXPLAIN THIS TO SNOWBIRD?
IT WAS ONLY YESTERDAY WHEN I WORKED UP THE COURAGE TO GO SEE HIM.
OLD MAN?
A-MI-NAY?
WHO'S THERE?
MAYBE I'M YOUR LONG-LOST GRANDSON, AND MAYBE I WANT TO MAKE MY LONG-LOST GRANDPA RICH.

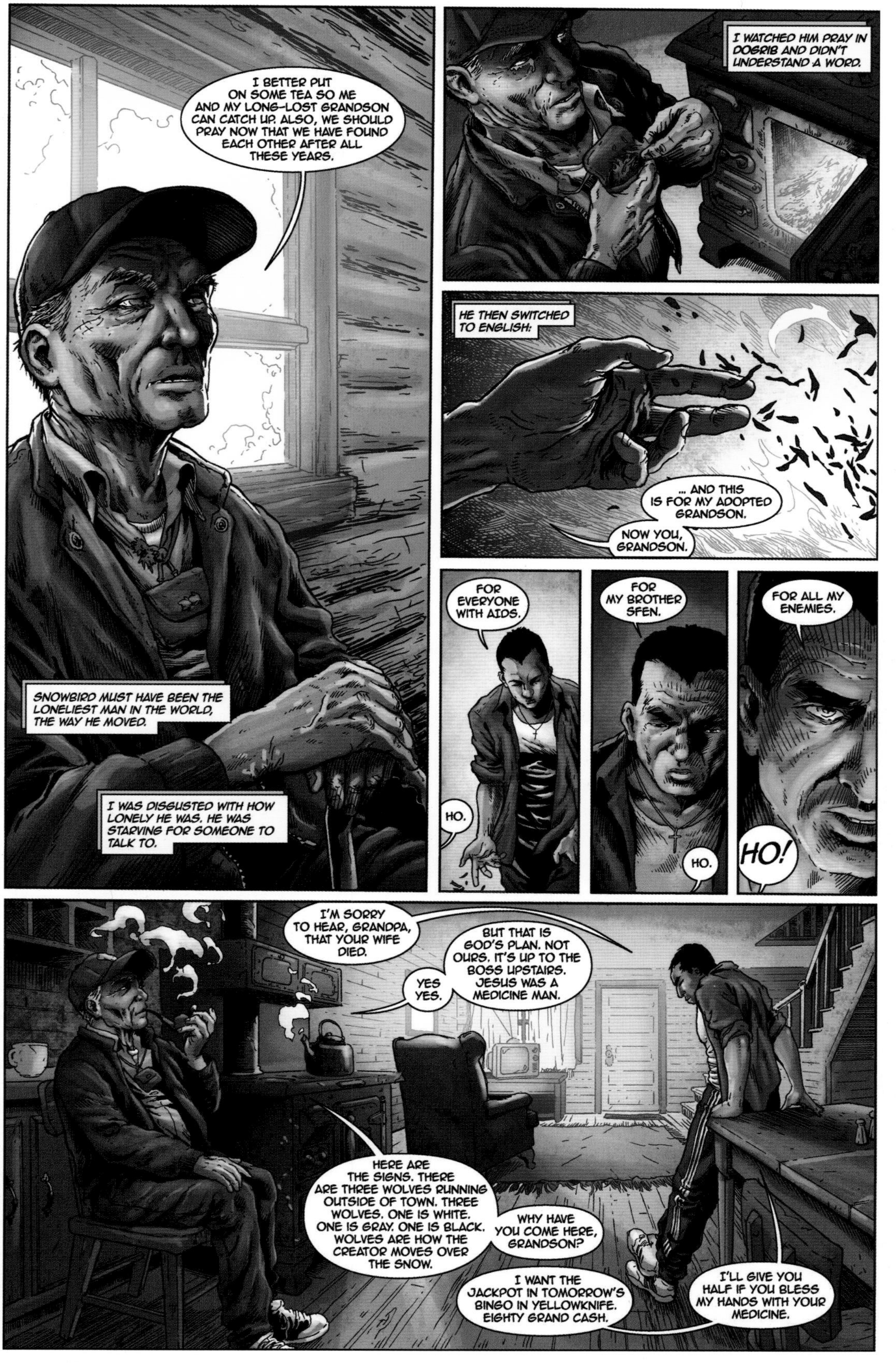
I BETTER PUT ON SOME TEA SO ME AND MY LONG-LOST GRANDSON CAN CATCH UP. ALSO, WE SHOULD PRAY NOW THAT WE HAVE FOUND EACH OTHER AFTER ALL THESE YEARS.
SNOWBIRD MUST HAVE BEEN THE LONELIEST MAN IN THE WORLD, THE WAY HE MOVED.
I WAS DISGUSTED WITH HOW LONELY HE WAS. HE WAS STARVING FOR SOMEONE TO TALK TO.
I WATCHED HIM PRAY IN DOGRIB AND DIDN'T UNDERSTAND A WORD.
HE THEN SWITCHED TO ENGLISH:
... AND THIS IS FOR MY ADOPTED GRANDSON.
NOW YOU, GRANDSON.
FOR EVERYONE WITH AIDS.
HO.
FOR MY BROTHER SFEN.
HO.
FOR ALL MY ENEMIES.
HO!
I'M SORRY TO HEAR, GRANDPA, THAT YOUR WIFE DIED.
YES YES.
BUT THAT IS GOD'S PLAN. NOT OURS. IT'S UP TO THE BOSS UPSTAIRS. JESUS WAS A MEDICINE MAN.
HERE ARE THE SIGNS. THERE ARE THREE WOLVES RUNNING OUTSIDE OF TOWN. THREE WOLVES. ONE IS WHITE. ONE IS GRAY. ONE IS BLACK. WOLVES ARE HOW THE CREATOR MOVES OVER THE SNOW.
WHY HAVE YOU COME HERE, GRANDSON?
I WANT THE JACKPOT IN TOMORROW'S BINGO IN YELLOWKNIFE. EIGHTY GRAND CASH.
I'LL GIVE YOU HALF IF YOU BLESS MY HANDS WITH YOUR MEDICINE.

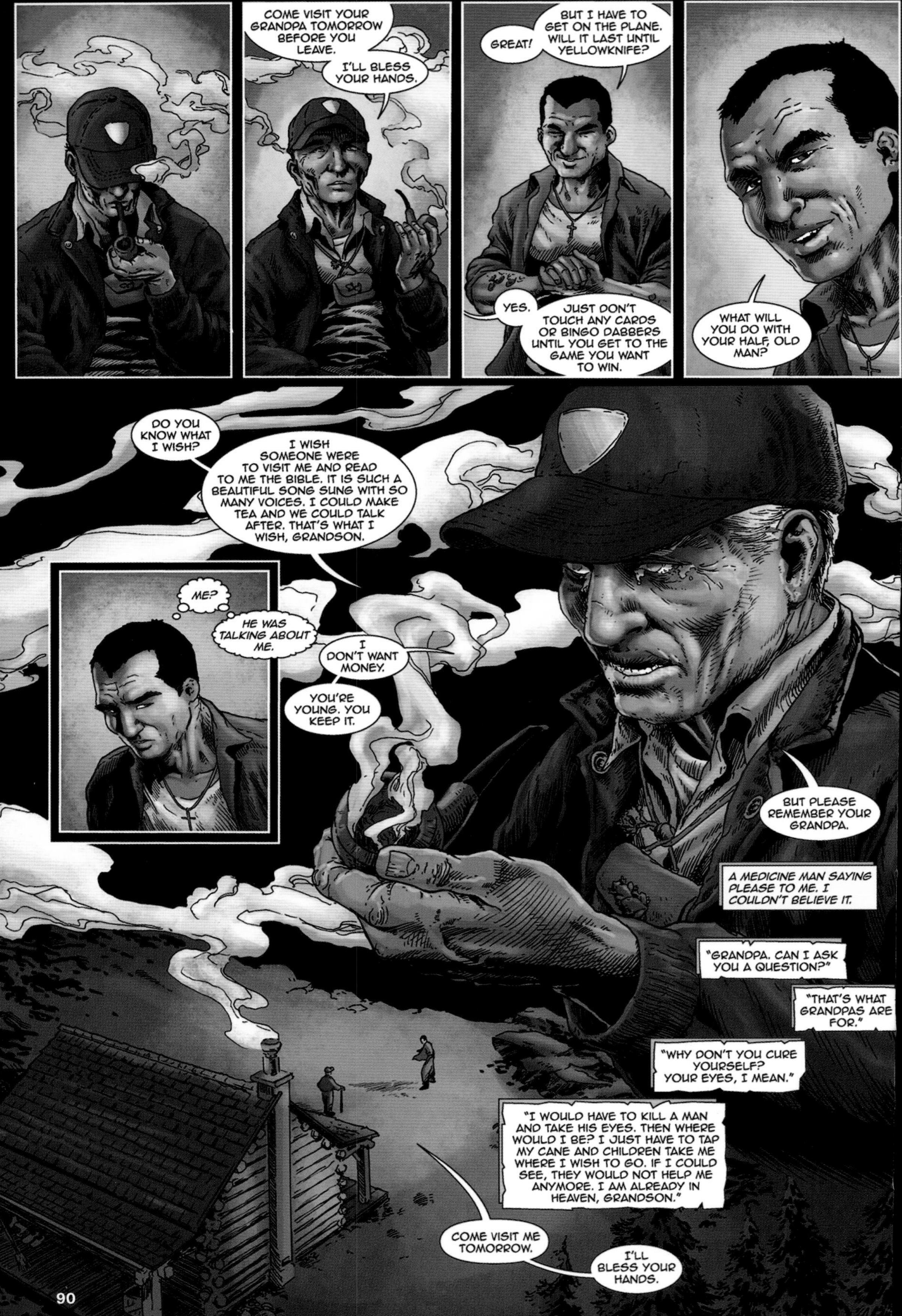
COME VISIT YOUR GRANDPA TOMORROW BEFORE YOU LEAVE.
I'LL BLESS YOUR HANDS.
GREAT!
BUT I HAVE TO GET ON THE PLANE. WILL IT LAST UNTIL YELLOWKNIFE?
YES.
JUST DON'T TOUCH ANY CARDS OR BINGO DABBERS UNTIL YOU GET TO THE GAME YOU WANT TO WIN.
WHAT WILL YOU DO WITH YOUR HALF, OLD MAN?
DO YOU KNOW WHAT I WISH?
I WISH SOMEONE WERE TO VISIT ME AND READ TO ME THE BIBLE. IT IS SUCH A BEAUTIFUL SONG SUNG WITH SO MANY VOICES. I COULD MAKE TEA AND WE COULD TALK AFTER. THAT'S WHAT I WISH, GRANDSON.
ME?
HE WAS TALKING ABOUT ME.
I DON'T WANT MONEY.
YOU'RE YOUNG. YOU KEEP IT.
BUT PLEASE REMEMBER YOUR GRANDPA.
A MEDICINE MAN SAYING PLEASE TO ME. I COULDN'T BELIEVE IT.
"GRANDPA. CAN I ASK YOU A QUESTION?"
"THAT'S WHAT GRANDPAS ARE FOR."
"WHY DON'T YOU CURE YOURSELF? YOUR EYES, I MEAN."
"I WOULD HAVE TO KILL A MAN AND TAKE HIS EYES. THEN WHERE WOULD I BE? I JUST HAVE TO TAP MY CANE AND CHILDREN TAKE ME WHERE I WISH TO GO. IF I COULD SEE, THEY WOULD NOT HELP ME ANYMORE. I AM ALREADY IN HEAVEN, GRANDSON."
COME VISIT ME TOMORROW.
I'LL BLESS YOUR HANDS.

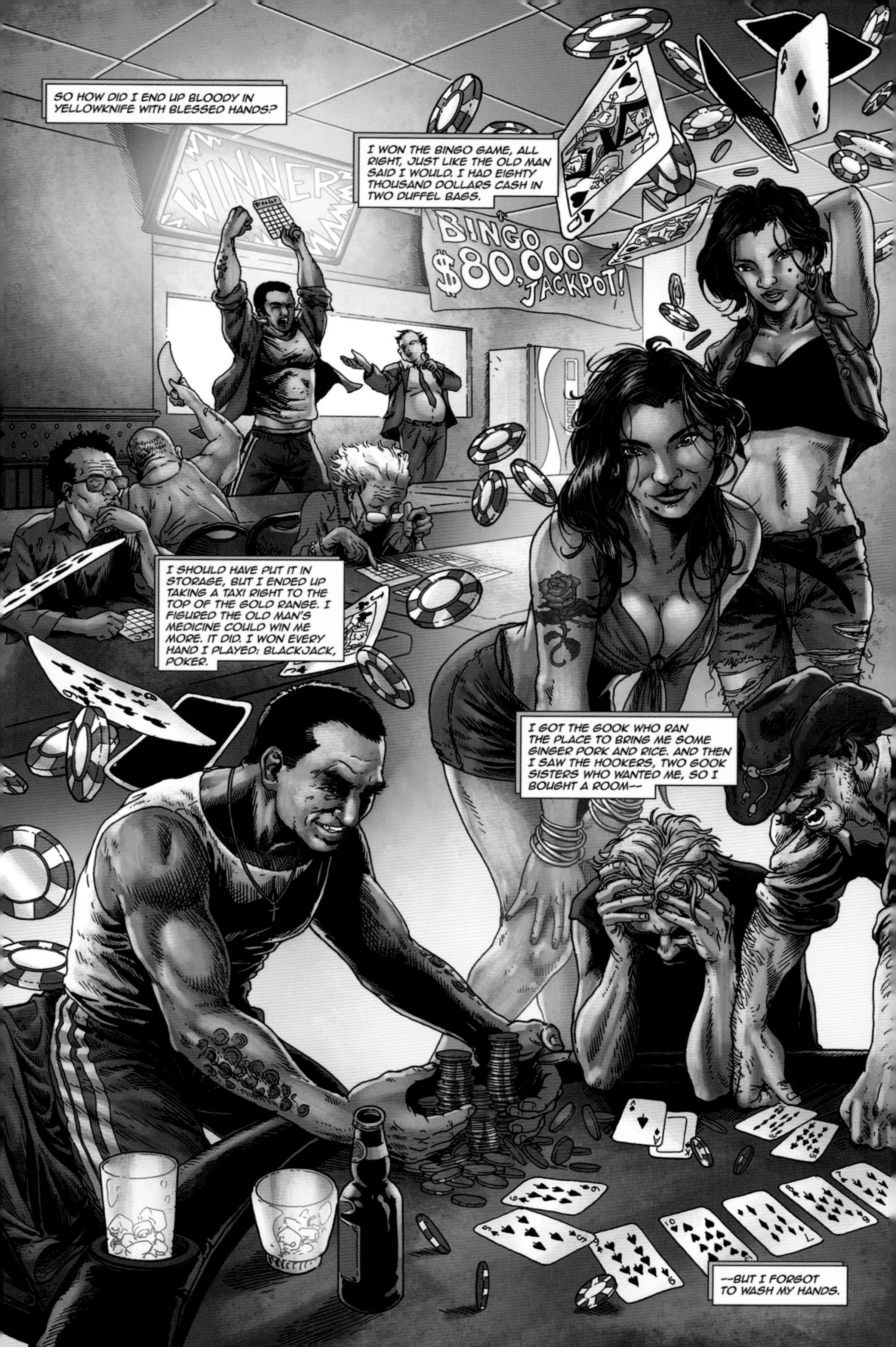
SO HOW DID I END UP BLOODY IN YELLOWKNIFE WITH BLESSED HANDS?
I WON THE BINGO GAME, ALL RIGHT, JUST LIKE THE OLD MAN SAID I WOULD. I HAD EIGHTY THOUSAND DOLLARS CASH IN TWO DUFFEL BAGS.
WINNER
BINGO $80,000 JACKPOT!
I SHOULD HAVE PUT IT IN STORAGE, BUT I ENDED UP TAKING A TAXI RIGHT TO THE TOP OF THE GOLD RANGE. I FIGURED THE OLD MAN'S MEDICINE COULD WIN ME MORE. IT DID. I WON EVERY HAND I PLAYED: BLACKJACK, POKER.
I GOT THE GOOK WHO RAN THE PLACE TO BRING ME SOME GINGER PORK AND RICE. AND THEN I SAW THE HOOKERS, TWO GOOK SISTERS WHO WANTED ME, SO I BOUGHT A ROOM--
--BUT I FORGOT TO WASH MY HANDS.

I WOKE UP CHOKING AFTER THROWING FIRE INTO BOTH TWINS.

I LOOKED FOR SOMEONE TO KILL.

NO ONE.

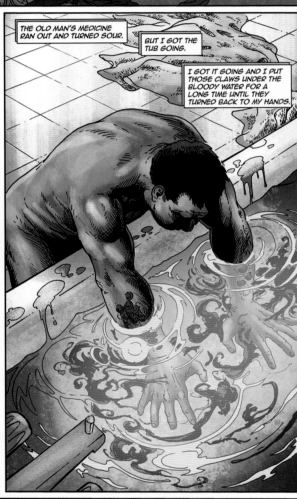

THE OLD MAN'S MEDICINE RAN OUT AND TURNED SOUR.

BUT I GOT THE TUB GOING.

I GOT IT GOING AND I PUT THOSE CLAWS UNDER THE BLOODY WATER FOR A LONG TIME UNTIL THEY TURNED BACK TO MY HANDS.

MY OWN HANDS WERE KILLING ME.

THE DEVIL'S CLAWS WERE ON ME.

WHEN I WENT BACK TO THE ROOM, THE TWINS HAD VANISHED WITH ALL MY MONEY.

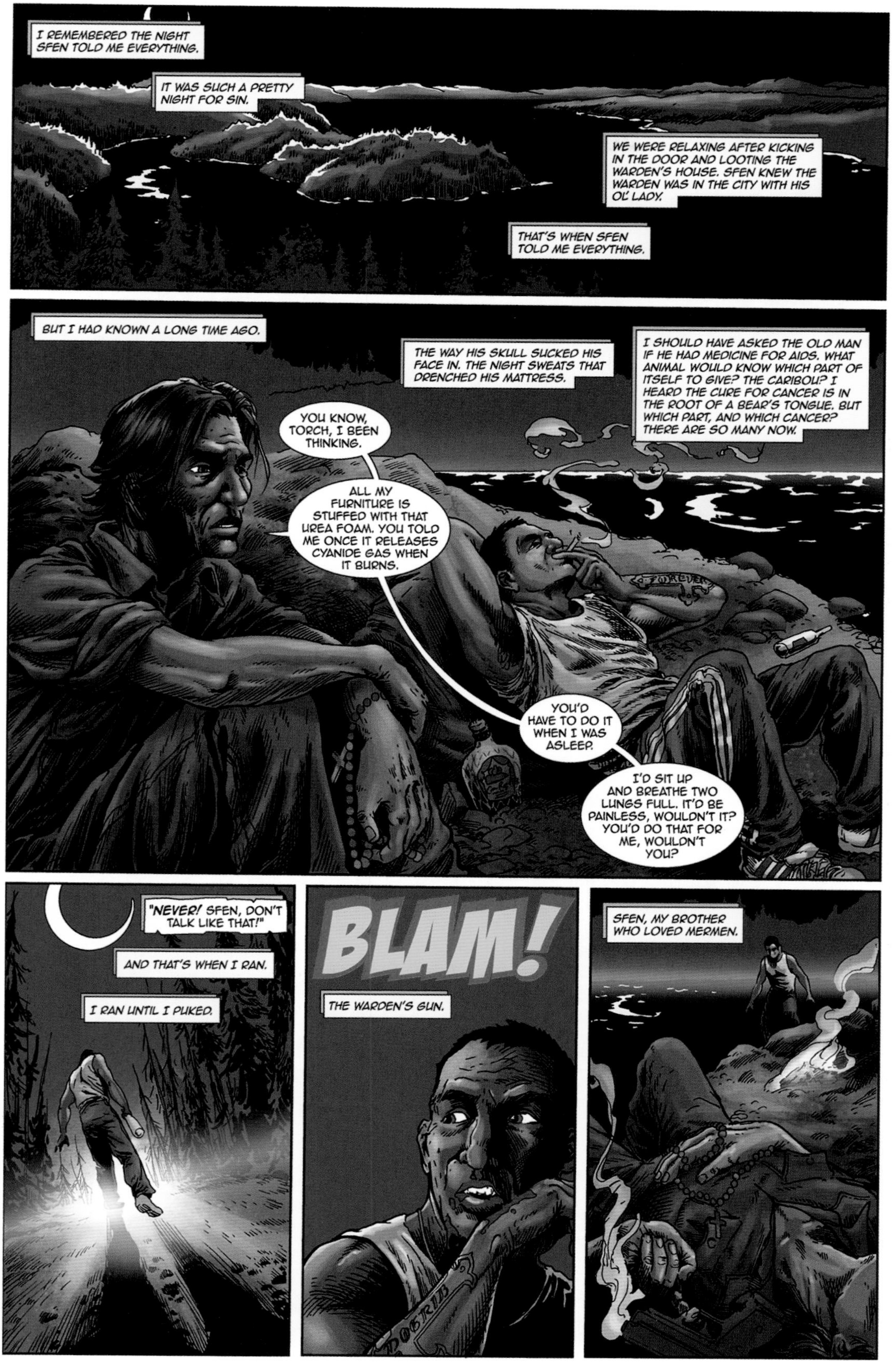
I REMEMBERED THE NIGHT SFEN TOLD ME EVERYTHING.
IT WAS SUCH A PRETTY NIGHT FOR SIN.
WE WERE RELAXING AFTER KICKING IN THE DOOR AND LOOTING THE WARDEN'S HOUSE. SFEN KNEW THE WARDEN WAS IN THE CITY WITH HIS OL' LADY.
THAT'S WHEN SFEN TOLD ME EVERYTHING.
BUT I HAD KNOWN A LONG TIME AGO.
THE WAY HIS SKULL SUCKED HIS FACE IN. THE NIGHT SWEATS THAT DRENCHED HIS MATTRESS.
I SHOULD HAVE ASKED THE OLD MAN IF HE HAD MEDICINE FOR AIDS. WHAT ANIMAL WOULD KNOW WHICH PART OF ITSELF TO GIVE? THE CARIBOU? I HEARD THE CURE FOR CANCER IS IN THE ROOT OF A BEAR'S TONGUE. BUT WHICH PART, AND WHICH CANCER? THERE ARE SO MANY NOW.
YOU KNOW, TORCH, I BEEN THINKING.
ALL MY FURNITURE IS STUFFED WITH THAT UREA FOAM. YOU TOLD ME ONCE IT RELEASES CYANIDE GAS WHEN IT BURNS.
YOU'D HAVE TO DO IT WHEN I WAS ASLEEP.
I'D SIT UP AND BREATHE TWO LUNGS FULL. IT'D BE PAINLESS, WOULDN'T IT? YOU'D DO THAT FOR ME, WOULDN'T YOU?
"NEVER! SFEN, DON'T TALK LIKE THAT!"
AND THAT'S WHEN I RAN.
I RAN UNTIL I PUKED.
BLAM!
THE WARDEN'S GUN.
SFEN, MY BROTHER WHO LOVED MERMEN.

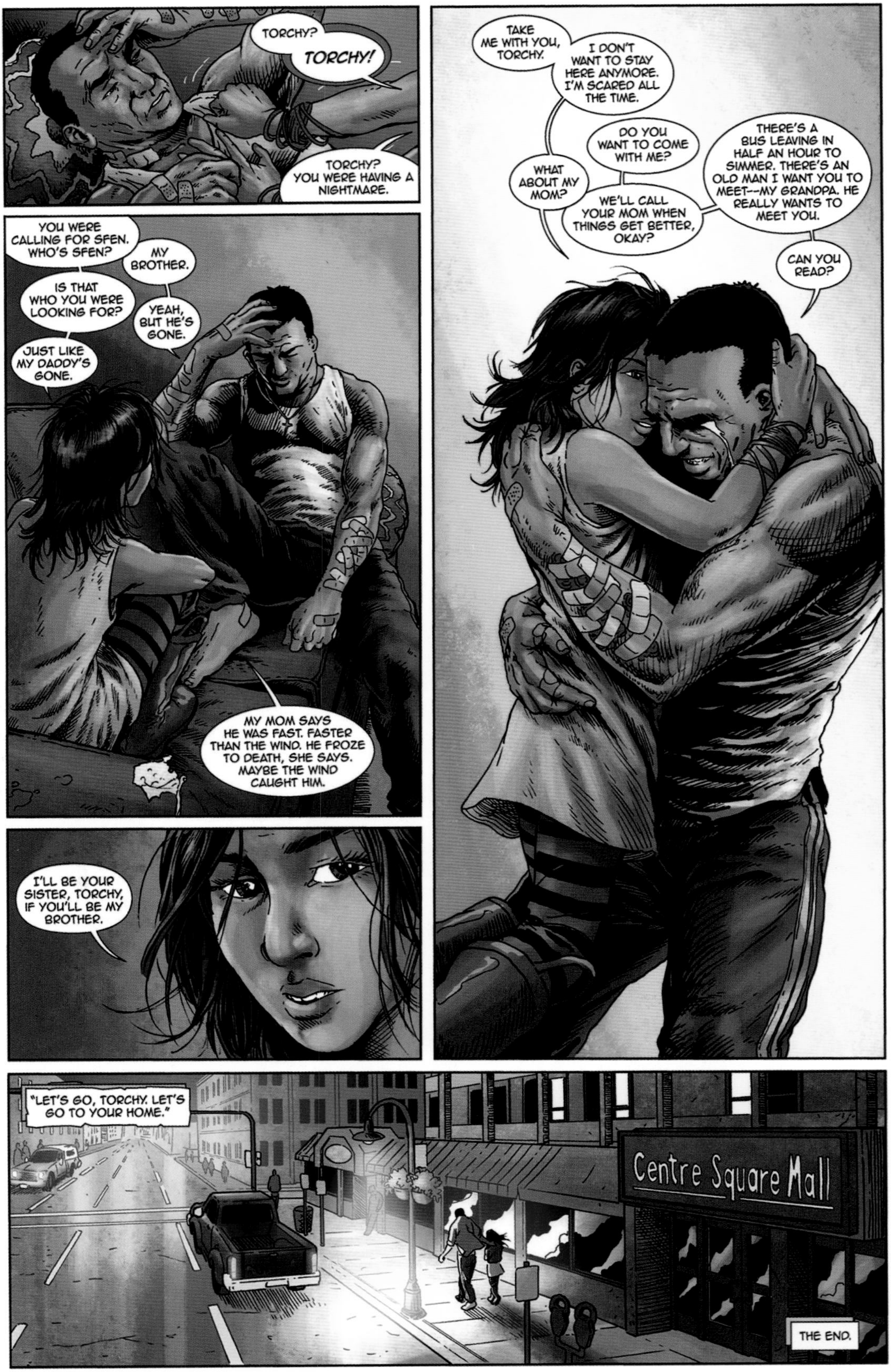
TORCHY?
TORCHY!
TORCHY? YOU WERE HAVING A NIGHTMARE.
YOU WERE CALLING FOR SFEN. WHO'S SFEN?
MY BROTHER.
IS THAT WHO YOU WERE LOOKING FOR?
YEAH, BUT HE'S GONE.
JUST LIKE MY DADDY'S GONE.
MY MOM SAYS HE WAS FAST. FASTER THAN THE WIND. HE FROZE TO DEATH, SHE SAYS. MAYBE THE WIND CAUGHT HIM.
I'LL BE YOUR SISTER, TORCHY, IF YOU'LL BE MY BROTHER.
TAKE ME WITH YOU, TORCHY.
I DON'T WANT TO STAY HERE ANYMORE. I'M SCARED ALL THE TIME.
DO YOU WANT TO COME WITH ME?
WHAT ABOUT MY MOM?
WE'LL CALL YOUR MOM WHEN THINGS GET BETTER, OKAY?
THERE'S A BUS LEAVING IN HALF AN HOUR TO SIMMER. THERE'S AN OLD MAN I WANT YOU TO MEET--MY GRANDPA. HE REALLY WANTS TO MEET YOU.
CAN YOU READ?
"LET'S GO, TORCHY. LET'S GO TO YOUR HOME."
Centre Square Mall
THE END.

Just Another Naming Ceremony

Gwen Nell Westerman

ILLUSTRATION & COLORS: Tara Ogaick

Gwen Nell Westerman is an enrolled member of the Sisseton-Wahpeton Dakota Oyate and an award-winning fiber artist. She is the coauthor of *Mni Sota Makoce: The Land of the Dakota*, which won a 2013 Minnesota Book Award. She has also published *Follow the Blackbirds*, a collection of poetry in Dakota and English. She teaches American Literature, Technical Communication, American Indian Literature, and the Humanities at Minnesota State University, Mankato. She received the Douglas R. Moore Faculty Research Award for her work in Dakota history and language.

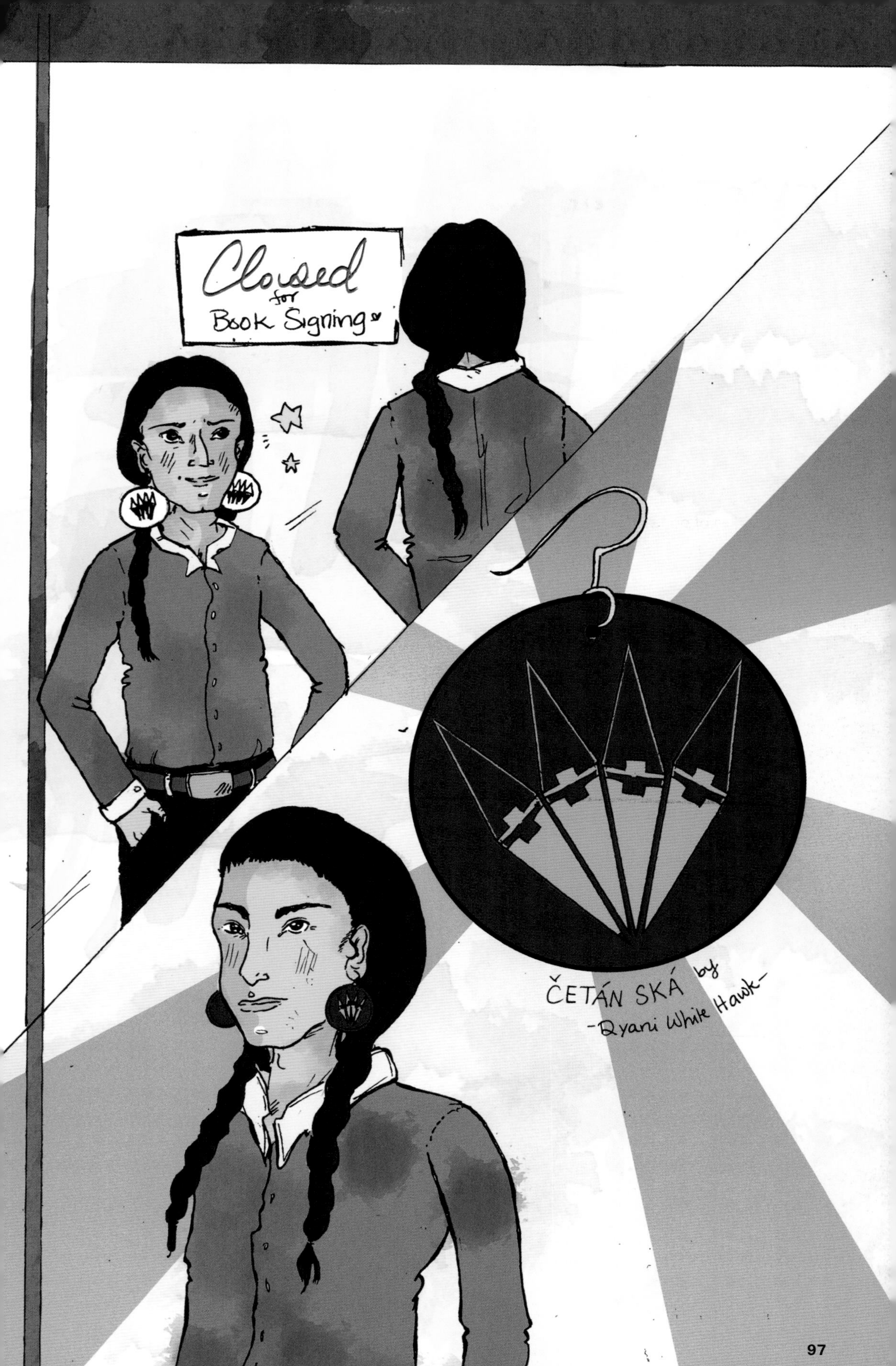
Closed for Book Signing
ČETÁN SKÁ by
-Qyani White Hawk-

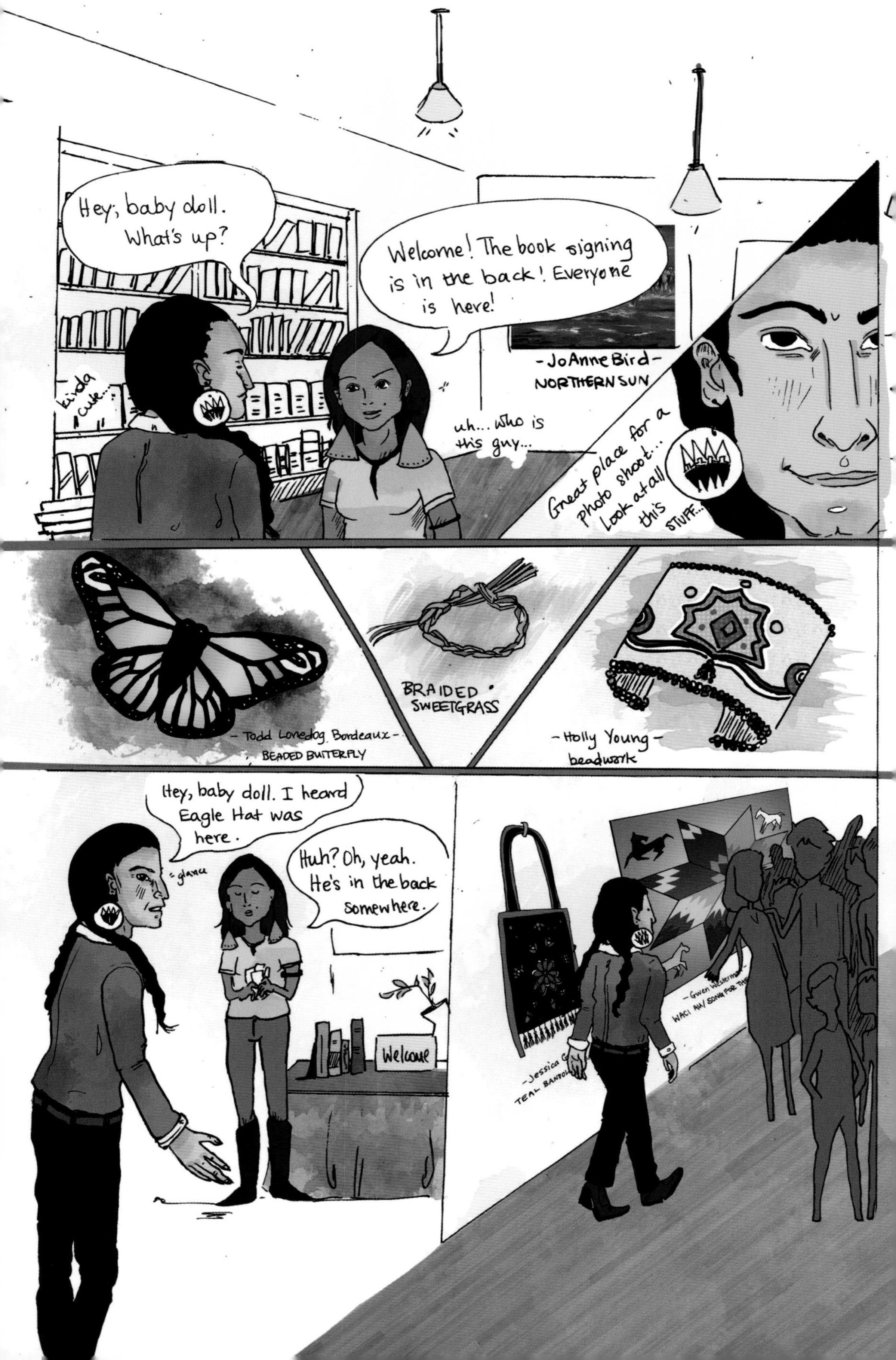

Hey; baby doll. What's up?
kinda cute...
Welcome! The book signing is in the back! Everyone is here!
uh... who is this guy...
-JoAnne Bird-
NORTHERN SUN
Great place for a photo shoot... Look at all this STUFF...
BRAIDED SWEETGRASS
-Todd Lonedog Bordeaux-
BEADED BUTTERFLY
-Holly Young-
beadwork
Hey, baby doll. I heard Eagle Hat was here.
glance
Huh? Oh, yeah. He's in the back somewhere.
Welcome

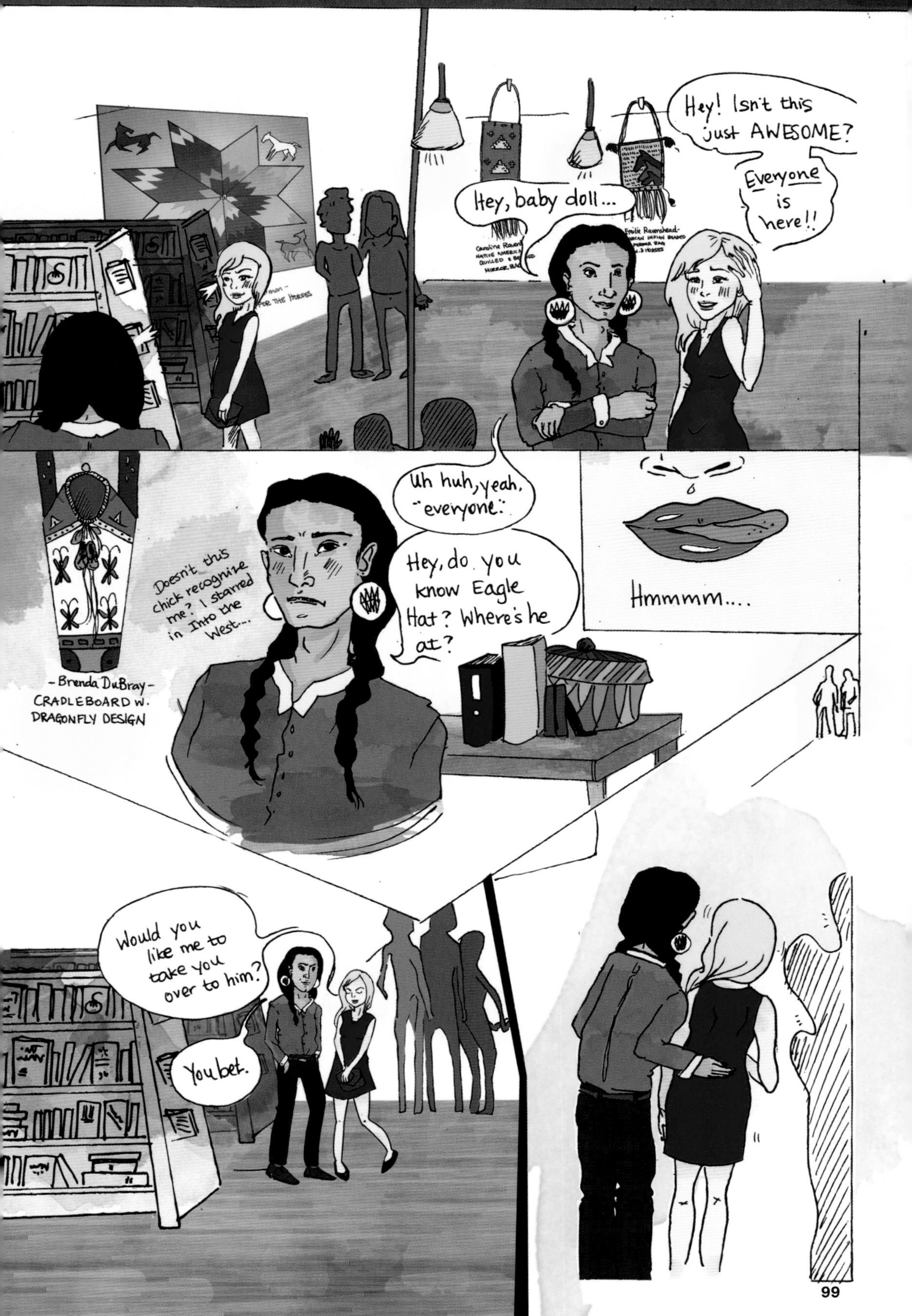

Hey, baby doll...
Hey! Isn't this just AWESOME?
Everyone is here!!
- Brenda DuBray -
CRADLEBOARD W. DRAGONFLY DESIGN
Doesn't this chick recognize me? I starred in Into the West...
Uh huh, yeah, "everyone."
Hey, do you know Eagle Hat? Where's he at?
Hmmmm....
Would you like me to take you over to him?
You bet.

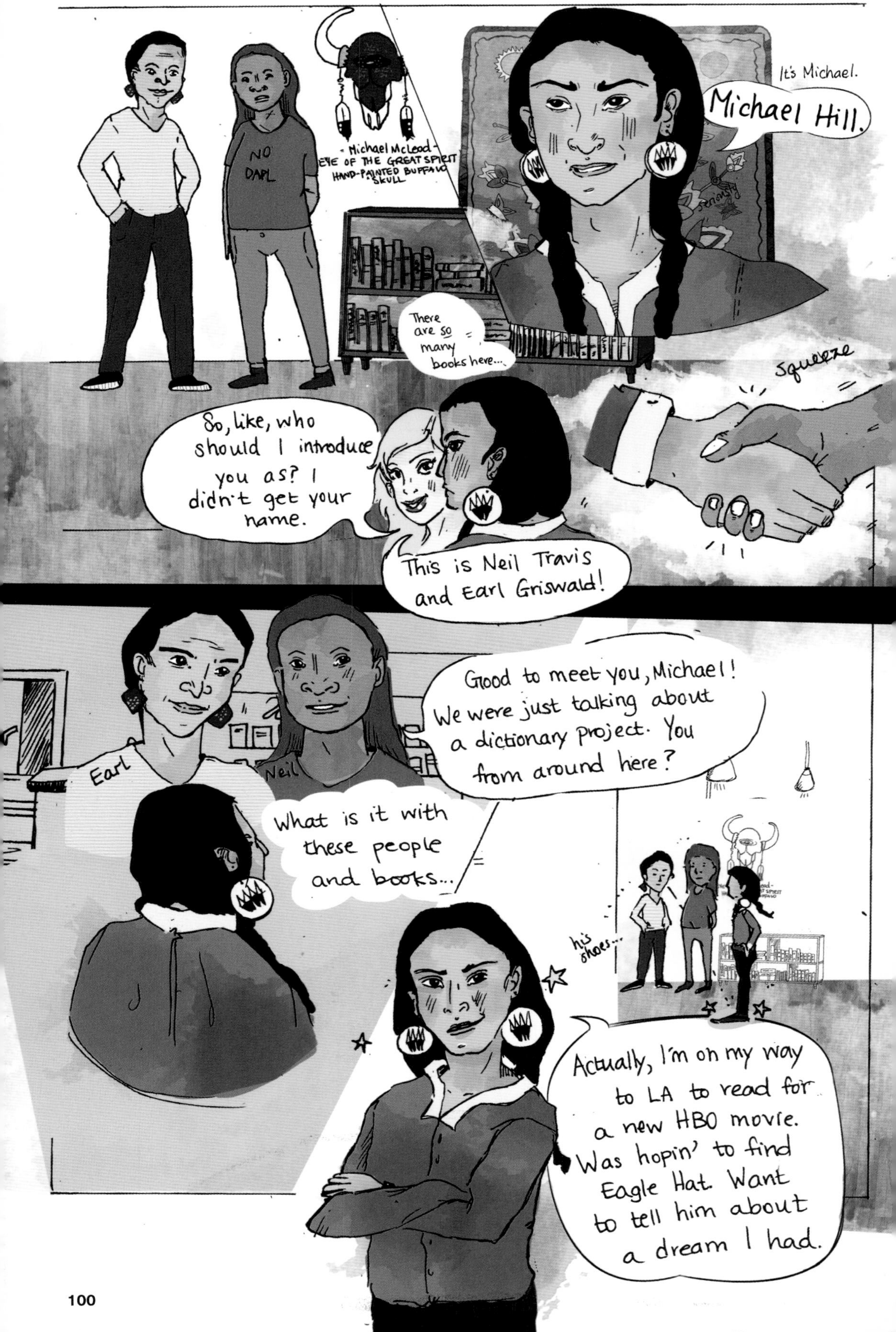

NO DAPL
- Michael McLeod -
EYE OF THE GREAT SPIRIT
HAND-PAINTED BUFFALO SKULL
It's Michael.
Michael Hill.
seriously
There are so many books here...
Squeeze
So, like, who should I introduce you as? I didn't get your name.
This is Neil Travis and Earl Griswald!
Earl
Neil
Good to meet you, Michael! We were just talking about a dictionary project. You from around here?
What is it with these people and books...
his shoes...
Actually, I'm on my way to LA to read for a new HBO movie. Was hopin' to find Eagle Hat. Want to tell him about a dream I had.

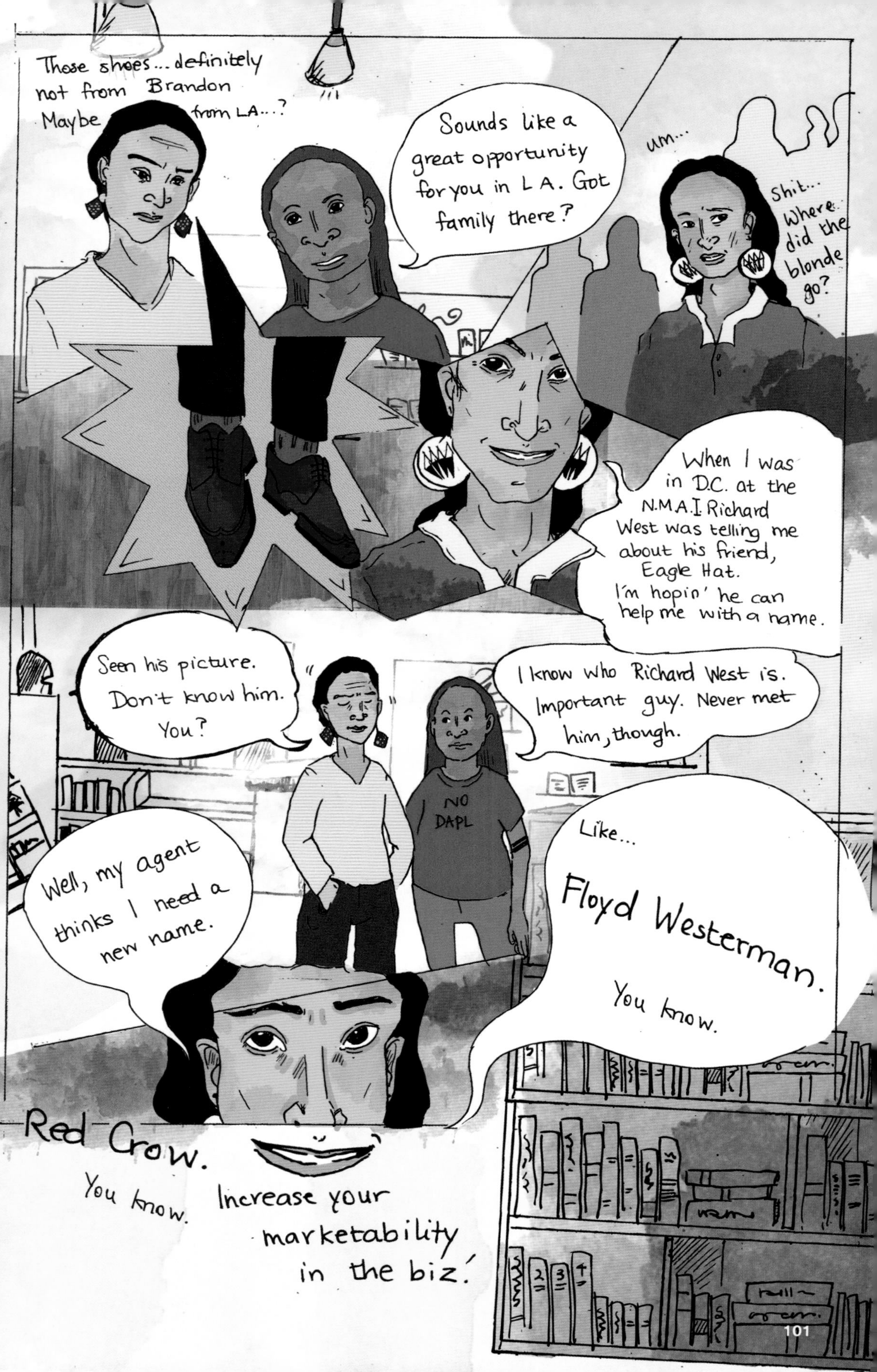
Those shoes... definitely not from Brandon
Maybe from LA...?
Sounds like a great opportunity for you in L A. Got family there?
um...
Shit... Where did the blonde go?
When I was in D.C. at the N.M.A.I. Richard West was telling me about his friend, Eagle Hat. I'm hopin' he can help me with a name.
Seen his picture. Don't know him. You?
I know who Richard West is. Important guy. Never met him, though.
NO DAPL
Well, my agent thinks I need a new name.
Like...
Floyd Westerman.
You know.
Red Crow.
You know.
Increase your marketability in the biz!

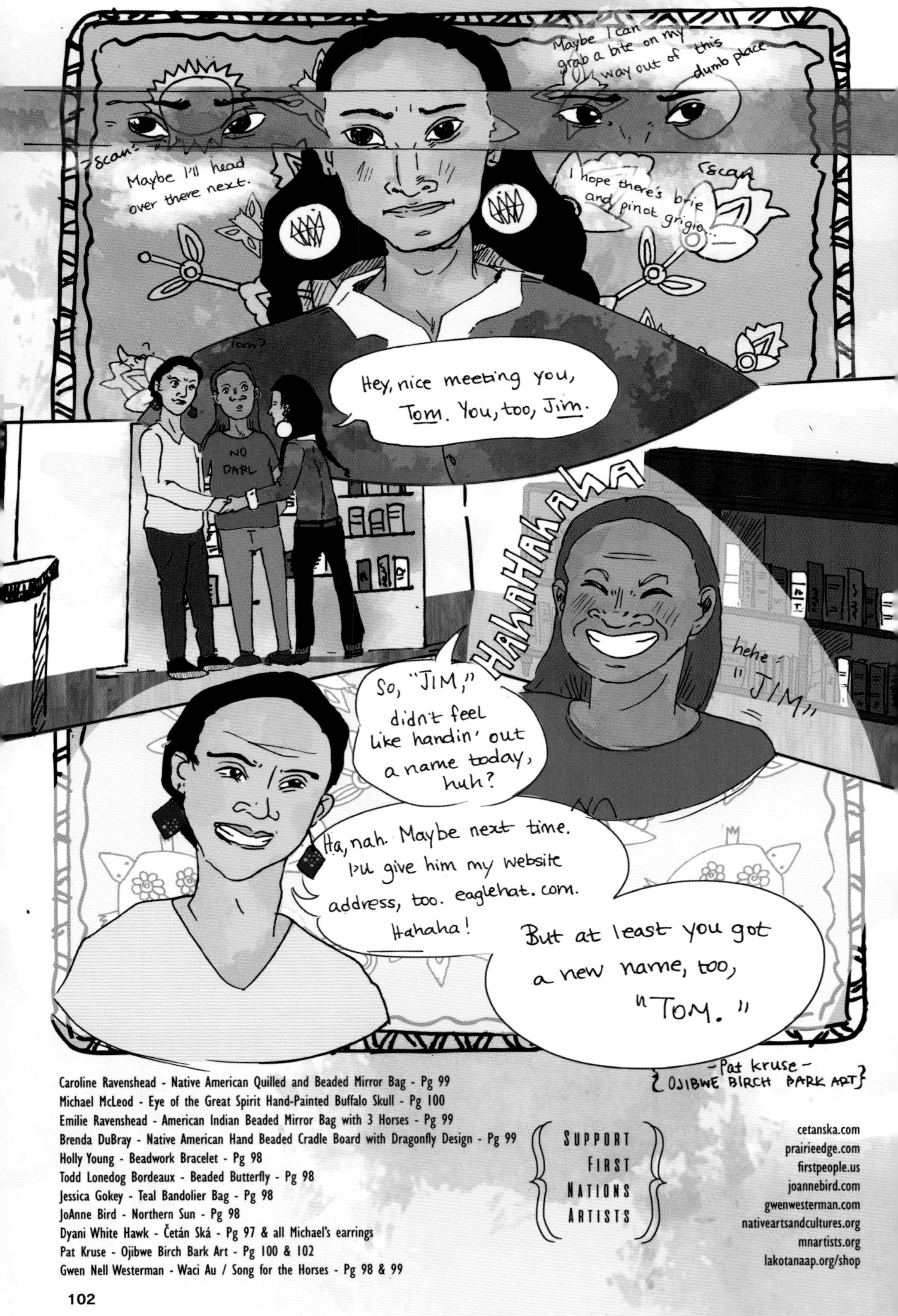
Maybe I can grab a bite on my way out of this dumb place.
scan
Maybe I'll head over there next.
scan
I hope there's brie and pinot grigio...
Tom?
Hey, nice meeting you, Tom. You, too, Jim.
NO DAPL
HAHAHAHAHA
So, "JIM," didn't feel like handin' out a name today, huh?
hehe "JIM"
Ha, nah. Maybe next time. I'll give him my website address, too. eaglehat.com. Hahaha!
But at least you got a new name, too, "TOM."
-Pat kruse-
{OJIBWE BIRCH BARK ART}

Caroline Ravenshead - Native American Quilled and Beaded Mirror Bag - Pg 99
Michael McLeod - Eye of the Great Spirit Hand-Painted Buffalo Skull - Pg 100
Emilie Ravenshead - American Indian Beaded Mirror Bag with 3 Horses - Pg 99
Brenda DuBray - Native American Hand Beaded Cradle Board with Dragonfly Design - Pg 99
Holly Young - Beadwork Bracelet - Pg 98
Todd Lonedog Bordeaux - Beaded Butterfly - Pg 98
Jessica Gokey - Teal Bandolier Bag - Pg 98
JoAnne Bird - Northern Sun - Pg 98
Dyani White Hawk - Četán Ská - Pg 97 & all Michael's earrings
Pat Kruse - Ojibwe Birch Bark Art - Pg 100 & 102
Gwen Nell Westerman - Waci Au / Song for the Horses - Pg 98 & 99

{ SUPPORT FIRST NATIONS ARTISTS }

cetanska.com
prairieedge.com
firstpeople.us
joannebird.com
gwenwesterman.com
nativeartsandcultures.org
mnartists.org
lakotanaap.org/shop

about the editors

Gordon Henry Jr. is an enrolled member of the White Earth Anishinaabe Nation in Minnesota. Dr. Henry also is a Professor in the English Department at Michigan State University, where he teaches American Indian Literature, Creative Writing, and courses in the Integrative Arts and Humanities. He serves as Series Editor of the American Indian Studies Series (and the series sub-imprint Makwa Enewed) at Michigan State University Press. Under his editorship the AISS has published research and creative work by an array of scholars, working in a variety of disciplines. Six years ago, while serving as Director of the Native American Institute at Michigan State, he, along with Ellen Cushman, founded the Native American Youth Film Institute. As an offshoot of that project Professor Henry is working with the NAI and the Michigan Inter-Tribal Council, on Indigistory, a community based digital storytelling project. Gordon also is a published poet and fiction writer. In 1995 he received an American Book Award for his novel *The Light People* and his poetry, fiction, and essays have been published extensively, in the United States and Europe. In 2004 he co-published an educational reader on Ojibwe people with George Cornell. In 2007 he published a mixed-genre collection, titled *The Failure of Certain Charms*. He also co-edited a collection of essays on American Indian Literature, titled *Stories through Theories/Theories through Stories* in 2009. His poetry, fiction, and critical writing has been published extensively internationally. His writing has appeared in journals and anthologies, and in translation in Spain, Greece, Hungary, Italy, the U.K., and Germany. Professor Henry is currently a Gordon Russell Visiting Professor at Dartmouth College, where he is teaching courses in Re-mapping Tribal Narratives and the American Indian Novel.

Elizabeth LaPensée, Ph.D., is an award-winning designer, writer, artist, and researcher who creates and studies Indigenous-led media such as games and comics. She is Anishinaabe from Baawaating, with relations at Bay Mills Indian Community, and Métis. She is currently an Assistant Professor of Media and Information and Writing, Rhetoric and American Cultures at Michigan State University. She started writing for comics in 2008, when two of her stories were supported by Aboriginal Peoples Television Network's Comic Creation Nation. She contributed to the award-winning *MOONSHOT: The Indigenous Comics Collection Series*. She wrote *Deer Woman: A Vignette* (2015) which led to her coediting *Deer Woman: An Anthology* (2017), a collection by Indigenous women illustrators and writers.